ROAD RAGE
the A - Z of motorist's safety

ROAD RAGE
the A - Z of motorist's safety

Graham Yuill, *ADI*

Otter Publications
Chichester, England

First published in 1996 by **Otter Publications**, 5 Mosse Gardens, Fishbourne, Chichester, West Sussex, PO19 3PQ.

DISCLAIMER
Whilst the information herein is supplied in good faith, no responsibility is taken by either the publisher or the author for any damage, injury or loss, however caused, which may arise from the use of the information provided.

WARNING
Do not attempt any of the manoeuvres without the supervision of a Department of Transport Approved Driving Instructor who specialises in evasive and awareness driving skills.

British Library Cataloging in Publication Data
A CIP record for this book is available from the British Library.
ISBN 1 899053 10 7

Acknowledgements
The section on drinking and driving is reproduced from Wheels of Justice - the motorist's guide to the law, by Duncan Callow. The extracts regarding caravans, are reproduced from information leaflets with the kind permission of the Caravan Club, East Grinstead House, East Grinstead, West Sussex, RH19 1UA.

Text design by Angela Hutchings.
Cover design by Jim Wilkie.
All cartoons by Simon Golding.
Printed and bound in Great Britain by Hartnolls Ltd., Bodmin.
Distributed in the UK by Grantham Book Services, Isaac Newton Way, Alma Park Industrial Estate, Grantham, Lincolnshire, NG31 9SD.
The Otter Publications logo is reproduced from original artwork by David Kitt.

CONTENTS

FOREWORD

With the ever increasing communication opportunities, media coverage and tremendous day to day pressures that most of us have to endure, it is hardly surprising that violence on the road is being singled out and the subject has even been given its own title - **Road Rage**. Each and every one of us as motorists, will have suffered frustration at some time or other. Only stringent attitudinal training and a will on the driver's part to remain cool during extreme provocation, will prevent even the wary motorist from being locked into confrontation. We visit our dentist regularly for a check up, but when was the last time you heard of somebody dying from tooth decay? Road users on the other hand, are killed in their thousands and therefore I urge you to get back to your professional driving instructor and take some advanced driver training, or if you are that good already, apply for the DIAmond Advanced Motorists Driving Test. In this way there will be an opportunity for you to promote the practice of chivalry into our everyday motoring.

Good luck and safe driving.

Graham R. J. Fryer
Chief Executive
DIAmond Advanced Motorists

PART ONE

SAFETY FOR YOU
AND YOUR CAR

Chapter 1

Road Rage - Its
Causes And Effects

Driving is an art. It requires concentration, patience and a responsible attitude. To gain these qualities, you must adopt from the outset a safe disposition to your driving. This means being aware of your own personal and vehicular limitations, traffic rules, laws of the road, and consideration for the feelings of other road users, including pedestrians. Remember, a motor vehicle is not a toy, and in the hands of an irresponsible person is a lethal and dangerous weapon. Drivers who are inclined to gamble their lives to gain a few seconds, or those ill-mannered individuals who always want to be the driver in front and are willing to take silly risks to get there, or get irritated at other road users for simply just being there, or wage a one-man war against anyone wishing to overtake them, are participating in the disturbing widespread phenomenon 'Road Rage' or mad drivers disease.

Driving standards are affected by the way we live our lives, and the pressures on drivers to keep to strict timetables can cause great stress in the car. There is also a great deal less courtesy and consideration to other road users than some years ago, which is another aspect of road rage. By comparison there has been a universal deterioration in people's attitudes in society, and this is reflected in driving behaviour.

Most road rage offenders are perfectly normal human beings who have no criminal record of violence. There is beyond doubt a barbaric streak deep inside some drivers that ignites when they get behind the wheel. This irrational driving behaviour can be influenced by driving in congested town or city traffic, which is an ideal breeding ground for road rage. During normal driving, our stress levels increase and this stress accumulates when drivers worry needlessly that their vehicle may get stuck in a traffic jam, another vehicle may crash into it or it may break down. Before anything happens, drivers have already got themselves in a state of anxiety and when something does occur, they're primed to explode into a psychopathic road warrior. The ten most common causes of road rage are:

- Aggressive tailgating.
- Angry headlight flashing.
- Making obscene gestures.
- Deliberately obstructing other vehicles.
- Giving verbal abuse.
- Unnecessary centre or outer lane cruising.
- Driving too slowly.
- Emerging or cutting in front of closely approaching traffic.
- Not signalling where necessary.
- Angry horn tooting.

Here are some do's and don'ts for reducing road rage risks:

Do:
- Forget the row you had with your spouse over the burnt toast/the business of the day, and concentrate on your driving.
- Lock your doors to avoid unauthorised entry.
- Try and stay calm if you're provoked by another driver.
- Avoid eye contact with your aggressor.
- Attempt to drive away from the scene if your crazed assailant approaches your vehicle to avoid further confrontation.
- Take a note of your aggressors registration number and report the incident to the police as soon as possible.
- Take extra breaks on long journeys if you are prone to road rage.
- Put your radio or CD player on to distract you in tense situations such as traffic jams.
- Count from one to ten to stop you leaping out of your vehicle in a blind rage.
- Show courtesy to other drivers which can calm ruffled tempers.
- Acknowledge your driving faults by apologising to the other driver.
- See a psychiatrist if you cannot control your road rage.

Don't:
- Make rude gestures to your assailant.
- Get even if you are assaulted.
- Overreact to what is already a tense situation.
- Carry items in your car that could be used as a dangerous weapon.
- Shout or bawl if you are provoked.

- Challenge your aggressor if you are confronted.
- Leave the safety of you vehicle if you sense trouble.
- Threaten your aggressor.
- Retaliate by slamming on your brakes suddenly, flashing lights or horn beeping.
- Goad your assailant into vehicle combat.

The Rights Of A Victim After Attack

SELF-DEFENCE
The law states that anyone who is attacked is entitled to ward off the assailant by **reasonable** means for his own protection. It is not always necessary for the attacker to strike the first blow if physical aggression is reasonably feared. The force must not **exceed** what is required to beat off the attack. However, if the attack is made with such extreme violence that the victim's life is in danger, it may be justified even to kill the assailant as a last resort. In all cases, no hard or fast rules of law apply. The court has to decide whether in all the circumstances the forces used were **reasonable**.

"You are charged with the use of excessive force, with a Woman's Own! How do you plead?"

OFFENSIVE WEAPONS

In olden days, horsemen would protect themselves by riding on the left-hand side of the road, close to thick-wooded hedgerows. Since the majority of people were right-handed, they would draw their swords with their right hands in order to defend themselves if they were attacked by the enemy. However, it is now an offence to carry a sword or other offensive weapon in your car for self-defence. In fact it is illegal to carry anything in your car capable of causing injury without having a lawful reason.

USING YOUR CAR AS A WEAPON

Most people do not consider a car to be an offensive weapon. This is because it is a familiar everyday object which is taken for granted and is only perceived as being an offensive weapon when someone becomes involved in an accident. However, a motor vehicle is not a toy and in the hands of an idiot it is indeed a dangerous and lethal weapon.

THE MINI-MAGLITE® FLASHLIGHT

A friend of mine once struck someone on the head with a Mini-Maglite® flashlight, (which was attached to his car keys), in self-defence. He was later charged with possessing an offensive weapon. However, his case did not go to court. Although the Mini-Maglite® flashlight had been used in the attack, there was no evidence that it had originally been carried for that purpose.

The Mini-Maglite® flashlight can be used as a very effective self-defence weapon and it can also be used to restrain very violent attackers. One end has a hole drilled through it so that a key ring may be attached to it. You can use the Mini-Maglite® flashlight to poke, apply pressure or strike an opponent. Always keep your Mini-Maglite® flashlight attached to your car keys. At night, you can use your Mini-Maglite® flashlight to check your car before getting into it.

Chapter 2

Recognising Attacks

Always remember that you can be attacked and physically assaulted at any place and at any time of the day when you are driving your car. This chapter aims to teach you how to recognise attacks before they become deadly emergencies.

DO NOT PANIC

Always remember that once an attack happens the odds are in the favour of the assailant. The secret is not to panic. Panicking is sudden and infectious fear. To avoid panicking, you must be trained to react positively with controlled aggression. When an attack does happen, you normally have split seconds to respond. If you sit and do nothing, recovering from the shock or contemplating what to do, you are at the mercy of the attacker. In a few seconds, a good driver can get himself out of any trouble.

THE SNATCH TECHNIQUE

Many attacks will take place in or near the victim's motor car. Let us look at a typical "snatch" technique used by attackers. Imagine that the victim's car is travelling along the road and suddenly a vehicle pulls out of a side road which causes the victim to execute an emergency stop. The car travelling behind the victim's vehicle will then most probably crash into the rear, so adding to the crisis, or it will effectively block its rear. The assailants will then storm the victim's car, assaulting or knocking out anyone who poses a threat to them.

The victim may then be forced out of the car and abducted or beaten up and perhaps dumped at the side of the road. The incident will happen very quickly and the site for the attack will be well chosen. There will be few, if any, witnesses (see figure 1).

There are five **fatal** mistakes a driver can make when an attack happens.

THE FIVE FATAL MISTAKES
1. *Complacency*

This mistake occurs when a driver travels on the same road, carrying out the same routine day after day. This leads the driver into a false sense of security as he will be "switched off", assuming that danger will never happen. Should an attack occur, the driver's response will be much longer, as he must mentally work out in his head how to react in order to deal with the situation correctly rather than this simply being a "reflex" action.

Victim's car

Figure 1. The Snatch Technique.

2. *Not reacting*

Your attacker will not expect you to react positively if an attack happens. It could be a car-jacker or opportunist thief attempting to rob you of your possessions. It may even be a sex attacker or murderer trying to rape or kill you. By not reacting, you have played right into your assailant's hands.

3. *No escape route*

Imagine driving through traffic and the vehicle in front of you stops at a set of traffic lights. If you do not leave enough distance from the vehicle in front of you when you stop, another driver travelling behind you could position his car close to your rear bumper and you will be boxed in. Never get caught in between two vehicles. Anything could happen and you will be trapped with no escape route if you are attacked. A good driver always stops his vehicle a safe distance from the vehicle in front (See figure 2).

4. *Vehicle location*
You can be at your most vulnerable if you have to reverse your car out of a drive way or from a parking space. This would give you less time to drive out of danger. It is therefore prudent to reverse into a drive way or parking space for a quick getaway.

5. *Vehicle skills*
Quite clearly, if the driver has not been properly trained in evasive and awareness driving skills then he will not be able to react properly should an attack happen.

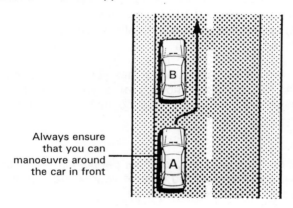

Always ensure
that you can
manoeuvre around
the car in front

Figure 2. Always keep a safe distance from the vehicle in front.

RECOGNISING THE RISK
It is important to recognise and anticipate an attack before it happens (e.g. you should constantly be checking your mirrors and side roads). Most attacks could be avoided if it were possible to realise the imminent danger and react just one second earlier. On the other hand, you must be aware that many approaches can be totally innocent - for instance, someone may just want to ask you for directions! You should watch the person's eyes and hands this is a true indication of their intentions.

YOU THE VICTIM
If someone has singled you out for an attack, he will most probably place you under surveillance. He will be watching your routines and may well build up a personality profile on you. The type of details that might be included in a personality profile are as follows:

- Date and place of birth.
- Home and business addresses.
- Family history and spouse's background.
- University or college attended.
- Military or police service.
- Business directorships and shareholdings.
- Type of employment and business contacts.
- Income.
- Property details.
- Hobbies and regular meeting places.
- Membership of any political party and position held.
- Type of vehicle(s) owned and most commonly driven.
- Details of close friends.

If you discover that someone is enquiring into your background in areas such as these, without your knowing of a valid reason, you should immediately be on your guard and contact the appropriate authorities.

KEEPING SAFE
If you are setting out on a long journey, let other people know the route you are going to take and the expected time of your arrival. Here are some other measures you can take to keep safe:

- Ensure that the car is maintained in good condition. Check the tyres, brakes and steering at the start of every journey.
- Always carry a personal alarm (obtainable from DIY shops) whilst driving and keep it where you can get access to it easily. Don't leave it at the bottom of your handbag.
- Keep a map in the car to avoid getting lost or having to ask directions, or else use an in-car or hand-held route finder. When you program your destination into the route finder it will provide you with the quickest route, it will re-route you round any traffic jam, and it will also calculate the estimated time of your arrival. This is a very useful in-car navigation aid; it enables motorist's to reach their destination safely and with the minimum amount of fuss.
- Keep the rear parcel shelf free from loose objects. This will prevent any chance of injury to passengers during any enforced emergency stop.

- Ensure that the windscreen is free from smears, check that the windscreen wipers are in good condition, and that the windscreen wash is topped up. All these measures will prevent accidents.
- Make sure that the headlights are properly adjusted. This will maximise your own vision and minimise dazzle to others.
- Never leave children alone in your vehicle. A child can easily release a parking brake or open a door.
- Always have a torch in your car.
- If you stop for petrol or for a break, take your keys with you and check the rear seat when returning to your car (someone may have climbed into the back).
- When you return to your car, study it first to see if it has been tampered with. If it has, and you sense danger, leave your car alone and inform the police immediately.
- Make sure that you have your car keys ready so that you can enter your vehicle quickly. When you get into your car lock your doors immediately even when carrying a baby or holding an object.
- Remember that if your car has central locking it will unlock all the doors. Look around for any dubious-looking characters near your car before you use it.
- Avoid parking where there are hedges and walls.
- At night, always park your car in a well-lit street.
- When you park your car in daylight, consider what the area will be like if you intend returning when it is dark.
- If you have to leave your car in a tiered car park (check when the car park closes), try to position your car in a well-lit area, as near as possible to the ground floor, near a ramp and the attendant's booth or as close to the entrance as possible.
- If it is within your means, purchase a mobile phone. Some companies now do a very low-price connection and rental for the infrequent user.
- If you see an emergency or an accident, drive on and inform the police as soon as possible.
- Make sure your fuel tank is full. If you run out of fuel, change into neutral and if it is safe use the momentum of the car to move to the side of the road in order to stop.
- Always carry spare fuel in a safe container and make sure you are a member of a well-known motoring organisation, in case your car breaks down.
- During wintery weather conditions, check the weather forecast.

- If your feet are wet, wipe them on the carpets or matting before driving your car, to prevent them from slipping off the foot pedals.
- Carry an advance warning triangle. It is simple to fold and easy to stow away.
- Carry jump leads in case you have to recharge your battery.
- In winter carry a flask containing a hot drink.
- Carry a de-icer and a window scraper.
- Never, under any circumstances, pick up a hitchhiker - even if they appear to be in distress. This could simply be a ploy. **Don't** be tempted to stop, even for harmless looking hitchhikers. Some attackers use a good-looking girl as bait to stop drivers. As soon as the driver stops his vehicle, muggers emerge from cover and storm the vehicle.
- Finally, many people sit on a cushion when they are driving to raise themselves up higher or for added comfort. However, recent tests have shown that this practice may increase the chances of being injured if a traffic accident occurs.

If your car does break down and you have to walk to get help, carry out the following procedures:

- Before you leave your car, take a note of its location.
- Place your warning triangle on a straight road, about 50 metres (55 yards), behind your car, on the road. If your car breaks down on a hilly or winding road, place the warning triangle where other drivers will see it in good time.
- Try to walk facing oncoming traffic so that no one can pull up behind you.
- If it is dark wear bright, preferably fluorescent, clothing or carry a torch so that a vehicle doesn't accidentally hit you. When there is no pavement and you have to walk on the road make sure that you keep as close to the verge as possible.
- Keep your distance from strangers (reaction space), as this will give you more time to react if you are attacked.
- Do not hitch-hike or take lifts from strangers.
- Avoid strangers by crossing the road.
- Cover up expensive-looking jewellery.
- Carry your handbag close to you in case someone grabs it.
- Keep your house keys and credit cards separate from your handbag.
- Don't take short cuts through dark alleys or across waste ground.

- If a car stops and you think someone is following you, cross the street to see if he is still tailing you. If the threat continues, don't be embarrassed to flag down a passing motorist. If you are attacked, pick up any solid object or take off your shoe so that you can smash a window and then scream for help. This will surprise your attacker and may frighten him away.
- Carry your screech alarm or a powerful whistle.
- Keep change and a phone card in case you have to call a garage or friend for help.
- Avoid standing near lonely bus stops, especially after dark.
- If you are mugged and your attacker is carrying a weapon, give the robber what he wants by emptying your handbag out on the ground and run away as quickly as possible.
- If you telephone for a taxi, be careful!

PERSONAL ALARMS

A personal alarm is designed to disorientate and surprise an attacker so that you can gain valuable seconds in which to escape (the noise can also attract other people's attention). You must take advantage of the time gained so that you can run *anywhere* that is safe. Always set your alarm off immediately if you are attacked. Thrust the alarm towards your attacker's head and aim it at his or her ear. Remember a personal alarm will only confuse your attacker for a few seconds. When you have beaten off the attack inform the police immediately. The description you give to the police about the attacker may help them catch the culprit before he strikes again.

THE PLUG-IN PORTABLE PHONE

Drivers can purchase a portable telephone that enables the user to summon help without leaving their car. By simply plugging the power lead into the cigarette lighter socket, services can be obtained by keying in a simple code. There is also a battery pack available for those vehicles that do not have a cigarette-lighter socket.

CAR PHONES

Do not use a mobile telephone whilst your vehicle is moving, unless in an emergency or if you are speaking into a hands-free unit. Many accidents are caused by drivers losing control of their vehicle because they are steering with only one hand on the wheel. There is another danger associated with mobile phones: under certain conditions it is possible for a mobile phone to cause a spark which could ignite petrol vapour, causing a fire or explosion, if it was being used in a petrol-filling station, for instance. Furthermore, safety researchers have discovered that hand-held phone sets could activate airbags if the car has them fitted.

In a recent survey carried out in the UK, 40% of car break-ins involve the theft of a mobile phone. To help the police link the phone with its true owner if it is stolen and subsequently recovered, you should mark your phone and battery with your initials and post code, and keep a note of its serial number in a secure place.

DANGEROUS AREAS

Always be on your guard if you return to your vehicle (especially in a dark street) and find a flat tyre on your car. Carefully look around before changing the wheel. Someone may have slashed the tyre and be waiting to attack you when your back is turned. They could also scatter black tacks on the road to puncture your tyres when you drive off. If you feel you could be in danger changing a flat tyre, first drive to a safer area. You can purchase an aerosol inflator and sealer to repair a flat tyre. This will save you time and effort having to change a wheel, so you can get to safety quickly.

MULTI-STOREY CAR PARKS

Many people, especially women, have been attacked in multi-storey car parks, even during daylight hours. Indoor car parks have become havens for criminals who find them to be an ideal place in which to steal, mug, or attack their victims, rather than out on the streets. Avoid parking (especially late at night) where there is poor lighting (including the stairs) or where the car park does not have closed circuit television or a security firm present. Attackers can easily hide in dark corners, behind parked vehicles or support pillars, under ramps, or stand silently in the murky shadows. After you have parked your vehicle, avoid sharing an elevator with any dubious-looking characters. It would be far safer to wait until someone else comes along whom you feel you can trust. If you see anyone acting suspiciously or ever feel unsafe, park somewhere else. If you have to pay to leave the car park, always have some change with you so you can get out quickly.

USING AN ELEVATOR

Always look into an elevator in a multi-storey car park before you enter. Do not enter if a dubious-looking person is in it. If a suspicious-looking character enters the elevator after you, avoid eye contact and make full use of peripheral vision. Stand by the control panel and press the button for the next floor and leave the lift if you sense trouble. Never enter an elevator on your own if it is bound for the basement and you are going up. Regard basements as potential danger. If you are in a building with several floors and you are attacked, you should press as many floor buttons as possible. When the lift stops at every level you can then scream for help. You should avoid pressing the alarm button because this will stop the lift and you will be trapped in the elevator with your attacker.

ACCEPTING A LIFT

You should always avoid accepting a lift from a stranger but if, for some pressing reason, this is unavoidable, it is a good idea to make sure you fail to shut the door properly so that you have to open it again. This will enable you to see how the door opens and whether there is a lock which has to be released first. If you smoke, light up a cigarette and be prepared to stab it in the driver's face (try and aim it at his eyes) if he attacks you. If you feel you may be in danger, leave the car quickly if it stops at traffic lights. You could also pretend you are feeling ill and that you are going to be sick. Put on an act and start burping then ask him to stop at the side of the road so that you can escape. If this subterfuge fails, you should consider more dramatic actions such as jerking the parking brake on or grabbing the steering wheel (in the road where it is reasonably safe to do so).

USING A TAXI

You should be extremely careful if you for any reason you have to abandon your car and telephone for a taxi. Many rapes by strangers reported in London involve mini-cabs. If you are phoning from a call box, don't let anyone hear you - someone may turn up later pretending to be a cab. Make sure you choose a reputable firm and ask the controller what colour or make of car will collect you, and the driver's name. When the taxi eventually arrives, make sure the driver identifies himself and gives your name, and sit in the rear of the cab. Try and avoid unnecessary conversation (do not tell the driver any personal details about yourself) and use body language to indicate that you are not interested if you are chatted up.

If you feel uncomfortable about the driver, order the taxi to stop at a busy area and get out. If you are travelling to somewhere where there is someone you know at home, it may be a sensible precaution to phone ahead so they'll expect your arrival. It is illegal for a non-hackney cab to pick up fares on the street. If a cab driver offers you a lift in this way, you should refuse and telephone for a cab from a firm you can trust. When you arrive at your destination, have your house keys ready and ask the driver to wait until you are safely inside.

UNMARKED POLICE VEHICLES

If another driver indicates that he wants you to stop your vehicle at the side of the road, you should avoid doing so unless you are positively sure that it is a police officer in an unmarked police car. The signs to look for are as follows:

1. Blue flashing lights.
2. Horns blaring.

After you have stopped, ensure you are shown official identification. The police officer must also state his name, his police station and the reason he has stopped you. Often, undercover police can deliberately be dubious-looking characters, without the standard short-back- and-sides haircuts, etc.

CAR JACKING

Car-jacking is a modern term which originated in the United States of America. In some states it became an epidemic. Women are usually the prime targets for the highwaymen who often work in gangs and surprise their victims when they are travelling alone. Attacks usually happen when the car has stopped at traffic lights. They approach their victims from a "blind spot" and sometimes assault them before making off with their valuables. The car-jackers sometimes target specific models of cars. The thugs force their victims out of their vehicles (sometimes using extreme violence) and then steal them. The robbers have calculated that, because of recent technological developments, modern cars are so well protected by sophisticated alarms and immobilisers that it is easier to try to steal them when they are on the move.

You can get an anti-hijack device fitted in your car; then if you are ever car-jacked, switch off the engine and abandon your vehicle (run away from the intruder) and permit the car-jacker to take your car. However, if the car-jacker does not key a code into the system he will be extremely disappointed when the anti-hijack device disables your vehicle shortly after he has driven away, and he may also be locked in the car.

A new device to counter the menace of joyriders is 'the stinger'. This is a hollow spiked device used by the police who fire the stinger across the road to burst the tyres of the vehicle to allow the vehicle to gradually come to a controlled stop.

DEALING WITH CAR-JACKERS

When you are driving in a busy area, it is highly probable that you will come across a set of traffic lights. Car-jackers often operate at traffic lights as the driver may have to stop and give way to pedestrians if the traffic lights are red. When driving, always scan the road ahead and to the side looking for any potential dangers. As you approach a set of traffic lights, you should be ready to accelerate out of danger should anyone attempt to force you to stop. If you have to stop at a set of traffic lights, watch out for anyone approaching your car (he may come from a "blind spot"). You are most at risk from car-jackers if you dress ostentatiously. *Remember*, **"If you've got it, be careful where you flaunt it"**. If someone approaches your car with the intention of speaking to you, carry out the following procedures:

- Make sure all your doors are locked.
- Keep your valuables out of sight.
- Under no circumstances unlock any of your doors.
- Pretend you are using your car telephone (authentic-looking dummy car telephones are also available).
- Lower your window only about 10 cm if he wants to speak to you. If you wind your window down too far he may grab you or punch you on the face.
- Do not switch your ignition off (you may have to drive off out of danger).
- If it is someone in plain clothes or in uniform claiming to be a police officer, ensure identification is produced and that you examine it.

Should he appear to be threatening you, consider "jumping" the traffic lights but only if it is safe for you to do so. If for any reason it is not possible for you to "jump" the traffic lights, carry out the following procedures:

- Keep calm and do not panic.
- Move to the centre of your car.

Consider using your horn or activate your panic alarm, in case the intruder smashes a window and opens any of the doors. Use the following equipment that you may have in your car to defend yourself, if necessary:

1. De-icer (you may have to shake the contents first).
2. Torch.

3. Hair/anti-perspirant spray.
4. Pen or pencil.
5. Metal nail file or comb.
6. Fire extinguisher.
7. Rolled up newspaper or magazine.
8. Mini-Maglite® flashlight.

Keep them all within easy reach. If you are attacked and you feel your life is in danger, try to aim at his eyes for maximum effect. Consider striking your attacker with your car door. Always use controlled aggression with speed. Should any of those techniques fail, you can carry out any of the following self-defence techniques:

Hair or ear grab
Grasp your attacker's hair. With enough aggression you can pull him all over the place and simultaneously strike him on the head with your Mini-Maglite® flashlight. If your attacker has short hair grab his ear.

Eye poke
It is impossible for anyone to build up the muscles in their eyes. To cause serious injury, poke him in the eyes with two fingers. Then follow up with another strike to the head with your Mini-Maglite® flashlight.

Throat grab
This is the most effective attack. Grasp the assailant's "throat" firmly and then quickly strike him with your Mini-Maglite® flashlight. You could also do a "karate chop" to the "throat".

BEING CAPTURED
If someone succeeds in entering your vehicle and forces you to drive to an area, you must know how to handle this frightening situation before you reach your assailant's planned destination, by which time it may be too late for you to react. Your attacker may threaten you with an offensive weapon or he may even grab your hair, shouting and threatening you with violence if you fail to comply with his instructions. Do exactly as your assailant tells you. However, if you feel your life is in danger, you should gradually build up the speed of your car until you reach a very fast speed. As soon as this happens, tighten your grip on the steering wheel, then slam on the footbrake as hard as possible (providing your attacker has not fastened his seat belt).

If you brake hard enough, your assailant will be projected forward very quickly and he will most probably be thrown through the windscreen or he may rebound back and forward off it, almost certainly knocking him unconscious or severely injuring him. You may have to endure some pain if your attacker has a good firm grip on your hair when he is being projected forward, although the shock of what is happening will probably make him release his grip. If your assailant has fastened his seat belt during the attack, don't worry but surreptitiously release his seat belt just before you brake very hard. His anchor point will be situated near your seat. Just make sure you choose his release button - **and not your own!**

After the attacker has been thrown from the car, you should speed away as quickly as possible. If your attacker is still inside your car, you should use your judgement as to whether it is better to push him from your vehicle or leave the vehicle and run. If the attacker is armed with an offensive weapon, it is probably best to get away from him immediately in case he lashes out at you; you should push him out only if you are sure he is definitely totally unconscious. If the area where you have stopped is populated, it will also be safer to leave the car and run towards help. If you feel you have to leave the car in an unpopulated area, try to grab the car keys before escaping or choose a route where a car could not pursue, e.g. over fences or across fields.

You or him
Always adopt a mental attitude of no mercy: a rapist or killer will show you none.

TAILGATING
Assume you are driving along and you see a vehicle behind driving too close to your bumper. If this happens to you, simply ease off the accelerator very gradually to ensure that he overtakes. If this subterfuge fails and you feel you may be in danger, stop your car as soon as possible at a safe place (e.g. a petrol station, shop, or pub). Put on your lights and continuously sound your horn very loudly and draw as much attention to yourself as possible.

BEING FOLLOWED
If you realise you are being followed, do not increase speed, even though you may be tempted to try and get away. If you speed up, the pest who is following you will suspect that you have noticed him and that you are afraid. If you sit comfortably, hold the steering wheel firmly, drive with confidence and stay calm as this may deter him. If possible, position your car so that your pursuer cannot drive alongside you. Act assertively and do not respond to any threatening behaviour. If you know the area and expect a left-hand turn ahead, turn without

signalling at the last possible moment or when your pursuer's car is just overtaking you. If you live alone, don't drive home. He may follow you to your front door or return later to pester you.

Chapter 3

Attack Counter-measures

Driving on your own, especially at night, can be a heart-pounding experience for many motorists, especially women. Many drivers feel vulnerable and unsure about the safest course of action to take if they are approached or attacked. This chapter deals with the precautions you can take to safeguard your vehicle and how to defend yourself when you are being attacked when driving your car.

HANG ON A SECOND!

TYPES OF ATTACKERS
Before we begin to look in detail at how you should keep safe behind the wheel of your car, you must understand that there are always men and women who are prepared to use violence to achieve their aim. Violence is a phenomenon which people naturally fear, as hardly a day passes without news of fatal assaults. The men and women who use violence, for whatever motive, can be classified into the following groups:

1. Opportunist (someone who does not plan an attack but may react to an "easy target").
2. Psychopath (mentally impaired individual, unable to stop killing).
3. Someone affected by drink or drugs (they have some effect on the brain and change the user's emotions or mental state).
4. Robber (someone who plunders or steals from another).
5. Sex attacker (most commonly strike at night).
6. Fanatic (someone who acts for a cause they are obsessive about, often a terrorist).

DRIVING AT NIGHT

If you are driving along a dark country road and you are forced by an attacker to stop your vehicle, you should carry out the following procedures:

- Immediately put on main beam and your spot lights.
- Activate your car alarm. This may cause the attacker to panic or it may attract attention if there is anyone in the vicinity.
- Grab your torch.
- Abandon your car.
- Move quickly into the shadows.

If you act very quickly, this can be a very effective technique, as your strong lights will momentarily blind your attacker which will give you enough time to escape.

USING A TORCH

It is a proven fact that using a strong light and loud noise simultaneously can disorientate an assailant. You can purchase several torches that have a very powerful beam and sirens capable of causing an attacker to panic and become disorientated when they are activated.

Attackers may also attempt to make use of torches. They may approach your car from behind, pointing the torch into your wing mirror so that you cannot watch what he is doing without being dazzled or he may appear at your side window, pointing the torch at your face, attempting to blind and disorientate you. The important thing is to avoid looking directly at the beam and follow the guidelines in this book.

ATTACK COUNTER-MEASURES

Here are some counter-measures that you can implement to avoid being attacked whilst driving:

- Try and travel with more than one person in the car.
- Close surveillance should be kept on accompanying traffic from the front and rear.
- Be particularly mindful of vehicles and motorbikes which draw up alongside you at traffic lights.
- Avoid opening your window more than 10 cm to prevent someone throwing a missile through the window.
- Beware of overtaking vehicles, especially on remote roads.
- Drive on major roads if possible.
- Consider using your car as a weapon if you are attacked.
- Always lock your doors to avoid unauthorised entry.
- Avoid routines. Vary your routes.
- Keep alert and be observant at all times.
- If you stop your vehicle in a situation where you feel unsure, do not turn off your engine as it may not start again.
- If another motorist attempts to make you stop by flashing their lights and indicating a fault on your car, acknowledge their signal, do not stop but drive to where you feel safe.

BEING RAMMED FROM BEHIND

If another driver crashes into the rear of your vehicle, you should use your judgement as to whether it is better to leave the safety of your car and exchange particulars with the other driver, signal the driver to follow you and proceed to a safe, well-lit area, or drive **immediately** to the nearest police station (try and record the other vehicle's registration number) and report the accident. You should **only** drive to the police station if you feel you may be in danger.

The police will be very sympathetic to you and will approve the course of action you have taken, especially if you are a lone woman driver. Some attackers use a stolen car so that they can ram the rear of another vehicle. As soon as the victim leaves the car the assailants will then attack the driver or anyone who poses a threat to them.

IF YOU HAVE BEEN ATTACKED
If someone seriously assaults or rapes you, contact the police as soon as possible. Do not wash or bath yourself until you have been examined by a doctor. Washing can destroy forensic evidence. Do not drink alcohol or take any tranquillisers in an attempt to calm your nerves. You will need to give the police a clear account of what happened.

Chapter 4

Protecting Your Vehicle

PREVENTING CAR THEFT

Some car thefts are carried out by determined professionals but the majority of cars are stolen by casual thieves who take advantage of an easy opportunity. A large proportion of car crimes are committed as a direct result of someone leaving a window open or a door unlocked. Do not hesitate in telephoning the police of any suspicious person tampering with your car. Give the police a description of the villain and **do not** attempt to challenge him ('have a go hero') as he may be carrying an offensive weapon or may be accompanied by someone else, possibly acting as a 'look out'.

A car's side windows are its weakest spot. A sharp tap with a blunt object will easily shatter them. To prevent this happening you can have your vehicle's side windows covered with a transparent laminated polyester film which is stuck to the inside of the side windows. Therefore, if the glass is struck from the outside, it will craze and not break. It will also inhibit a thief stealing from your car, and in the event of accident, glass fragments are held together to prevent cuts. The complete window can easily be pushed out, allowing the driver and passengers to escape.

You can get a series of electronic sensors built into either a door, the boot or even the bonnet; they trigger an alarm if any of them are forced open.

Some cars are protected by an engine immobilisation device. The car cannot start until the driver "punches" his personal code into a key pad. To de-activate the entire security system the driver simply presses a remote control button on a key fob. A stolen car can mean having to walk home late at night. Here are some precautions you can take to prevent your car from being stolen, and how to quickly recover your vehicle if someone takes it without your consent.

- Always lock your car, even when leaving your vehicle unattended for a few seconds.
- Never leave children alone in your car. Someone may abduct your child.
- Never place items of value in your car then leave your vehicle unattended. You never know who is watching you. If it is essential to leave something of value in the vehicle, ensure it is well hidden from view, i.e. in the boot.
- If your locks are worn, replace them.
- It would be a good investment to fit a good quality car alarm (make sure you use it at all times), or an immobiliser for extra security. A hidden cut-out switch can be cheaply fitted. You can also purchase an alarm which will activate when you press a button, either from inside or outside the car, as soon as someone attempts to steal it.
- You can get deadlocks fitted to the car doors so that they cannot be opened, even if the window has been broken.
- Whenever you leave your car always make sure that the steering lock has been engaged and that all the windows and doors are securely shut.
- To prevent your petrol tank from being siphoned, invest in a locking petrol cap and locking wheel nuts, to prevent expensive wheels and tyres from being stolen.
- You can purchase a car radio with a security code or one which can be removed every time you park.
- You can mark your car registration number of your vehicle on your car stereo or CD player with an ultra-violet (UV pen) that will show up only under ultra-violet light. This will help the police to trace the owner if they recover your goods.
- Never leave your driving licence, MOT certificate, registration document or insurance certificate in your car. These documents can help a thief to sell your car and provide a cover story if he or she is stopped by the police.
- Fit the most effective parking brake, gear lever or steering-wheel clamp.
- Have your windscreen, wing mirrors, lights and windows etched with your registration number.
- Always remove the ignition key, even if your car is in your garage. Some cars are fitted with a warning alarm to let you know if you leave your key in the ignition.
- When you park, watch out for strangers showing interest in your car; they may be planning to steal it rather than admiring it.

- Avoid parking in residential side streets or in unauthorised car parks.
- If you do not own a garage, park as close to your home as possible, preferably where you can see your car.
- If your vehicle is towing a caravan there are many security items on the market that you can purchase to help you protect your caravan. Crooks have been known to drive alongside an unprotected caravan, switch the van to their vehicle (usually stolen or with false number plates) and then drive off. The theft will happen very quickly.

STOLEN VEHICLE TRACKING SYSTEM

Recent technological developments allow you to get your vehicle fitted with a small transponder unit which is hidden in your car. You *don't* have to know where it is concealed. If your vehicle is stolen, you simply inform the police and the stolen vehicle tracking system control centre. The control centre instantly sends a unique coded signal to high-powered transmitters, which activates the transponder unit hidden in your car. This unit immediately starts broadcasting a silent homing signal. Police cars equipped with special tracking computers are alerted, and the signal leads them straight to your car, almost anywhere in the UK, even if it is hidden in a garage.

If you protect your car with the stolen vehicle tracking system there is an excellent chance that if your car is stolen it will be found very quickly, thereby dramatically reducing the risk and expense of theft, increased insurance premiums and the inconvenience of having no vehicle.

AERIAL/WING MIRRORS

When you park your car, always put the aerial fully down to stop it being vandalised. If you park your car in a narrow road and your car is fitted with spring loaded wing mirrors, you should consider tucking them in, to avoid them being 'ripped off' by passing motorists who have failed to give your vehicle sufficient clearance.

CARAVAN SECURITY

Over 2.000 caravans are stolen every year, and many are never returned to their original owners. They usually disappear into an illicit network of buyers and sellers, and when a caravan is eventually recovered by the police, all identifying marks have been removed. Occasionally the police must return the 'suspect' caravan to the thieves, simply because they cannot prove it belongs to someone else.

The majority of caravans are stolen from storage compounds closely followed by the owner's address. Thefts occur all year round and cover all ages of caravan, although newer models seem most vulnerable. To avoid becoming another insurance statistic, and to meet most insurers' conditions of acceptance, certain precautions should be taken.

There are many caravan security devices available on the market ranging from hitch locks to steady locks, from alarms to wheel clamps. Here is a list of security measures you can implement to prevent your caravan from being stolen and some advice on how to help the police recover it:

- Join The Caravan Club's Theftcheck scheme, by ensuring your caravan details are registered with them.
- Immobilise your caravan at all times, even when stopping for a short period.
- Consider a reliable alarm. The initial outlay is set against added security and peace of mind.
- Remove all personal belongings and contents from the caravan whenever it is not in use, and leave the curtains open, so potential thieves can see nothing of value is inside.
- Take a photograph of the caravan and keep it in a safe place, along with any registration documents. Make a note of any identifying marks or scratches.
- Mark the serial or chassis number in several places inside the caravan, using an ultra violet pen. Make a note of the mark locations.
- Ensure the chassis (VIN) number is etched on all the windows.
- Don't choose a storage site on price alone. Consider site security.

If the worst happens and the caravan is stolen, notify the police and insurance company immediately. Give the police a full description, including the chassis number and any identifying marks and contact Theftcheck as soon as possible so that the caravan details can be added to the register - it may help the police to quickly recover your caravan.

PART TWO

A - Z OF SAFETY
ON THE ROAD

"The life you save by good driving may one day be your own".
Graham Yuill, ADI

Chapter 5

Preventing Road Rage
And Other Motoring Tips

When driving, you often have to cope with unpredictable, irrational, offensive and quite often dangerous behaviour. To survive these conditions, it is imperative that you learn a defensive strategy. Driving instructors call this "defensive driving". This chapter teaches you defensive and evasive driving skills so that you can drive safely and survive on the road whilst driving and both avoid being a victim or sufferer of road rage!

A

ACCELERATOR STICKING DOWN
In many cases, this is due to a broken throttle return spring. Do not try to lift the pedal with your foot. Simply check the mirrors, change into neutral, switch off the ignition (but do not remove the ignition key as this will cause the steering wheel to lock), coast to the side of the road without crossing in front of any other vehicles, and stop.

AIRBAGS
Airbags are designed to protect you and your passengers in the event of a collision. Airbags are also installed on the front passenger's side in certain makes of cars. The driver's airbag is fitted in the centre of the steering wheel and it is designed to operate in the event of a significant frontal or front corner impact (about 18 mph), where the driver's head would otherwise hit the steering wheel, with the risk of serious injury. In the event of a serious crash the airbag will fully inflate in less than a second and it will make contact to protect the driver, then deflate to absorb the impact, again in less than a second after it has been activated.

ANIMALS IN THE STREET

If you are driving at speed, do not brake or swerve to avoid a dog or cat darting out in front of you if other vehicles are travelling closely behind you. The driver behind could run into your rear or you may even collide with oncoming traffic. It may seem cruel, but it is far safer to hit the animal even though this is the last thing you want to do. Many people have been seriously injured or killed when drivers have swerved suddenly to avoid a dog or cat.

Remember that if you are involved in an accident which causes injury or death to an animal (horse, cattle, ass, mule, sheep, pig, goat or dog) you must:

1. Stop.
2. Give details to anyone having reasonable grounds for requiring them, and,
3. If you do not do so at the time, report the accident to the Police within 24 hours.

ANTICIPATION

Since we now live in an age where violence against car drivers is on the increase, it is important to remember that you must never become complacent and you should be constantly vigilant against danger at all times when driving behind the wheel. This means expecting the unexpected and never being taken by surprise. You should question the actions of other road users and treat everyone as being potentially hostile until they prove otherwise. Always give yourself time and space so that you can anticipate the actions of other road users. A traffic accident may not be your fault, but fault will not be the issue for you if you are killed. If you drive with skill, anticipation and consideration for others, you need be neither its victim nor its perpetrator.

AVOIDING ACCIDENTS WHILST MANOEUVRING

Before reversing carry out all-round observations and give way to other road users because you will be travelling in the wrong direction. Turn well round in your seat and look out of the rear window. Reverse very slowly, particularly if people are standing nearby. Always remember before you reverse, it must be safe, legal and convenient. You may release your seat belt for ease of movement. A very important point to remember when reversing, is that you should always think which way your front wheels are pointing.

AVOIDING ACCIDENTS WITH PEDESTRIANS

Take account of pedestrians and animals, and be prepared to slow down or possibly stop if they run out in front of you without any warning. Elderly people who are less alert, need more time to cross the road; give them plenty of time. Never put them under pressure to cross the road quickly or leave them stranded in the middle of the road. Children are unpredictable, and they rely on you for their safety. Many children die in road accidents every year. The vast majority of these happen in built-up areas where the speed limits is 40 mph or less. Look out for people with white walking sticks or guide dogs. Remember that some people who are deaf or hard of hearing will not hear your car approaching (see figure 3).

Before turning a corner you must ensure that you "look" early as you approach the corner. If you start looking in good time you will be able to see any potential dangers in the road into which you are turning. Be especially mindful of pedestrians and give way to anyone who is ready to step off the pavement or has already stepped onto the road. Your vision may be restricted into your new road, and there will be a strong possibility that you may conflict with other traffic. Remember that, in addition, your vision may be obstructed by tall hedges, buildings, or parked vehicles. Before you turn, look in the direction that you intend your car to go, and make the turn neat, clean and sharp. As your car straightens up, it should stay parallel to the kerb. Do not swing inwards to the kerb or outwards to the centre of the road.

Figure 3. Give way to pedestrians.

You must always remember that once you have decided to turn into the corner, the speed of your car must be completely under control, and you must maintain the same speed throughout the corner. Accelerating into a corner too quickly is a dangerous practice. If your speed is not under complete control, you may cause your car to skid, or you may drive "blind" into some danger, without having time to brake. As soon as you are safely round the corner, cancel your indicator, (if necessary), check your mirrors and apply the accelerator, (conditions permitting), then select a good safety line position parallel with the new road. Remember, you must never accelerate if another vehicle is overtaking you.

AVOIDING UNDUE HESITANCY
Drivers often fail to make normal progress by undue hesitancy. For example, you are sitting at a "give way" junction waiting for a gap in the traffic to appear; a gap then appears but you do not take advantage of it and instead, decide to wait. You must not be overcautious to the point of becoming a nuisance. Try to keep your car moving at give way junctions if it is safe to do so. Give way junctions mean give way - they do not mean stop. Other drivers again may get frustrated and take silly risks to overtake you.

B

BONNET FLYING UP
Steer on the same course, braking progressively, signal and move carefully to the side of the road, again ensuring not to cut across any other vehicles. Winding down the driver's side window may assist forward vision.

BRAKES FAILING
Should your brakes suddenly fail, pump the brake pedal on and off and apply the parking brake quickly but progressively. Do not yank it. Start selecting lower gears to act as a brake on the engine. Run the edges of your wheels against the kerb. If you have time, beep your horn and switch on the lights to warn other road users of your presence.

BREAKING DOWN ON THE MOTORWAY
If your car breaks down whilst travelling on the motorway, move over to the hard shoulder at the earliest and safest opportunity. Try to cruise your car as far over to the verge as possible in case you have to repair a puncture on the driver's side of the car. Remember, the hard

shoulder is a very dangerous place to stop. Don't open any of the doors on the driver's side. Make sure you and all your passengers leave the vehicle from the passenger side and stand on the embankment away from the hard shoulder. Try to place your car as near as possible to an emergency telephone. Switch on your hazard lights to warn other drivers you have broken down. Position your warning triangle about 150 metres (165 yards) back from the car to warn other drivers.

Roadside markers may guide you to the whereabouts of the nearest emergency telephone. If someone approaches you whilst you are using the telephone (even if they appear genuine) give a description to the police at the control centre of what the person looks like and then take the registration number if he is driving a motor vehicle. Inform the stranger that you gave the police all his details. If he has criminal intent this will frighten him away. It has been known for motorists to be attacked and killed even in broad daylight near the hard shoulder. If for any reason it is not possible for you to reach an emergency telephone, you have the following options to chose from:

Option 1

Stay in your car, making sure it is as far away as possible from the carriageway. By doing this you will be less likely to be struck by other vehicles. Lock all doors to avoid unauthorised entry, and sit in the front passenger seat with your seat belt on in case your car is shunted from the rear. By sitting in the passenger seat you can give the impression that you are waiting for the driver to come back. It would be prudent to keep the lights on to enable other drivers to see you. The police or a major motoring organisation will eventually notice your predicament and come to your assistance, although you may have to wait for some time. It is highly advisable that you should join a major motoring association because they provide numerous services and usually arrive within the hour. The longer you have to wait at the side of the carriageway, the greater the danger you may be in.

Option 2

You may feel safer leaving your car and climbing over the barrier or up the bank at the side of the motorway. You can wait near your car but out of sight of passing motorists. Do not attempt to repair your car or cross to the other side of the motorway to use an emergency telephone - many accidents occur when other vehicles hit stationery vehicles on the hard shoulder. Leave the passenger door open and be ready to leap back in and lock the door behind you if another driver stops who, you feel, looks suspicious. It is a good idea to pack waterproof or extra warm clothing, spare boots and blankets before setting out on a long journey. You can use this spare clothing to keep you warm and dry should you have to wait for a long period of time. Stranded drivers (especially the disabled) should display a help pennant. A passing motorist may then alert the police or the emergency services. A person claiming to be from the emergency services should produce to you:

1. Proof of identification.
2. Your name.
3. The information you revealed to the control centre about the breakdown.

Remember judge each circumstance on its merit as there is no golden rule for all situations.

C

CARAVAN SAFETY
The need for safety on the road outweighs all other priorities. It is highly important that you carry out the following safety checks before setting out on a journey to ensure safe and trouble-free caravanning. Check:

- The caravan is carefully loaded to provide good balance and avoid instability As a general guide, the actual laden weight of your caravan should not exceed the kerb weight of the towing vehicle.
- Tyres (including spare) are free from cuts, bulges, blisters and have at least the minimum required tread depth of 1.6 mm.
- Both car and caravan tyres are inflated to the recommended pressure.
- Brake cables are properly connected and not damaged.
- Any parking/hand brake fitted works effectively.
- The coupling head on the trailer has engaged properly onto the towball.
- The breakaway cable is looped securely around the towing bracket, not just around the towball if at all possible.
- The number plate matches the towing vehicle (if this cannot be seen when towing) and can be illuminated after dark.
- The wheel nuts or bolts are correctly tightened to the appropriate torque setting.

- The load imposed by the trailer coupling on the towball does not exceed the vehicle manufacturer's limit.
- Any jockey wheel is clear of the ground and properly secured in this position.
- All road lights are working on the car and caravan.
- Walk around the outfit for a final check to make sure all is secure: corner steadies up, parking brake off, windows and roof lights closed, towball cover put away etc.
- The law requires the driver to have a good view to the rear, so you may need to fit additional mirrors to your car (but remove them when driving 'solo').
- Remember, it is illegal to allow passengers to travel inside the caravan. However, it is not illegal to carry animals, but it would be unwise to do so.

After twenty minutes, pull over and check:

- *Has a roof light blown open?*
- *Is everything in place inside the caravan?*
- *Has anything fallen onto the floor?*
- *Are the wheels cool? (If hot, you may have a binding brake).*
- *Are the tyres still properly inflated?*

Driving hints
When towing, everything takes a little longer than solo motoring so always apply good forward planning and anticipate the actions of other road users to avoid late and hurried driving decisions. By planning your driving in advance of any hazard and by signalling in good time and in a clear and unmistakeable manner you will be acknowledged as a considerate driver who does not allow his presence to impede the progress of other traffic.

Moreover, when towing a caravan, allowance should be made for the extra length and width when changing direction, overtaking or manoeuvring. Here are some driving hints to ensure a comfortable safe tow of your caravan.

- Overtaking and stopping distances increase when towing.
- Your caravan will be susceptible to side winds on exposed bridges and motorways and to bow waves set up by large vehicles, particularly when they are overtaking you or when you are overtaking them.

- Be aware of these potential hazards, make good use of your mirrors and watch your speed when travelling down hills.
- Until you are accustomed to the outfit, a maximum of 50 mph is advisable.
- You may travel at a maximum of 50 mph on signal carriageway roads, or 60 mph on dual carriageways and motorways unless a lower limit is in force.
- A safe speed is one at which the driver can stop under full control in a safe position on the road, well within the distance known to be clear.

Overtaking
When overtaking, you must be aware of the acceleration capability of your car so that you can move out of the 'danger period' as soon as possible. Look well ahead for oncoming traffic, junctions or hazards before you decide to overtake. Make effective use of your mirrors, and be particularly mindful of bicycles and motorcycles. Do **not** cut in too early after overtaking. *Remember the golden rule*; **If in doubt, DON'T**.

Turning right
Turning right in front of oncoming traffic requires patience and practice, allow yourself plenty of time for the manoeuvre, and take into account the length of your outfit. You should avoid cutting right-hand corners unless it is completely safe and absolutely necessary.

Reversing
Whilst reversing round a corner or into an opening, you should move your car very slowly and be prepared to give way to other road users including pedestrians. Remember, your initial movement of the steering wheel should be in the **opposite** direction to where you want the caravan to turn into.

Swaying
If the caravan starts to sway, to prevent the outfit becoming uncontrollable (a snake) you should ease off the accelerator gently to reduce your speed, trying not to brake at all. If you are gathering speed and must brake, do it **very gently** until the swaying has settled down. Do **not** try to fight the steering wheel, but keep it in the straight ahead position, as any sharp correction will worsen the swaying and may result in a 'snake'.

Avoiding road rage

Be considerate to other road users - never 'convoy', always leave space between yourself and another caravan or slow moving vehicle. If a queue has built up behind you, look for a safe place to pull in and let the traffic pass. Remember, you must not tow in the outside lane of a three or four lane motorway. Use the first lane, unless traffic is such that you would be constantly changing lanes to overtake. Under these circumstances you should stay in the second lane for longer periods and avoid the need to keep pulling out and cutting back.

Finally, I would strongly recommend that you join The Caravan Club. It is Europe's premier club for caravanners, motor caravanners and trailer tenters. They have a dedicated information department which will answer any queries relating to the purchase and use of a caravan, including advice on tow car capabilities, accessories and any legal or safety implications. The Club also runs practical courses for beginners or those wishing to improve their skills, and also offers insurance, finance, travel and road recovery packages for its members.

CARE IN THE USE OF SPEED

Speed is far and away the most common cause of death on the roads. A safe speed is one at which the driver can stop under full control in a safe position on the road, well within the distance known to be clear. Different types of weather conditions, the state of the road and any hazards on the road, will affect the speed of your car. You should slow down and make sure you can stop safely well within the distance you can see to be clear. If you are travelling on any roads outside built-up areas, it does not mean you can go as fast as you wish. You must obey the speed limits for the roads you are travelling on and the rules laid down in the Highway Code. Never accelerate into any hazard and be prepared to select a lower gear as the situation demands. A good driver always looks well ahead to avoid late and hurried driving decisions.

You must always drive at a speed that is safe, even though it may be lower than what is legal. The results of a survey have shown that more than half of car drivers killed die on country roads and often no other vehicle is involved. Pedestrians on country roads must often walk close to the side of the road where there is no pavement or footpath. Drive at a safe speed so that you do not endanger them should you meet opposing traffic. Likewise, drive slowly and carefully past animals. Give them plenty of room and do not frighten them by revving your engine or sounding your horn.

Exercising proper care in the use of speed will get you there even if it means arriving late. It is better to arrive late for an appointment than never to arrive at all. Imagine you are driving at 30 mph and you hit a little boy crossing the road. There is a 50/50 chance he will end up dead. If you hit him at 40 mph the chances of him surviving are virtually **nil**. *Remember*, **"Speed Kills"**; any wally can drive fast enough to be dangerous.

CHECK BLIND SPOTS BEFORE MOVING OFF AND OPENING DOORS

Presume you are parked at the left-hand side of the road. Before you can drive off from a stationary position, you must always check your interior and side mirrors. However, the mirrors do not scan the whole area, therefore there is a blind spot to your off-side, (right-hand side). To get round this problem you simply look over your right shoulder after you have checked your mirrors, before moving away. It is of vital importance to make these checks every time you decide to move off, in order to avoid a traffic accident (see figure 4).

Figure 4. Check blind spots before moving off.

COLLISION COURSE

If another driver falls asleep or loses control and his vehicle is heading straight towards you, you should sound your horn and flash your lights. Avoid driving onto the other side of the road, even if you think it is clear. The oncoming driver may wake up or gain control and pull left at the last moment. If you have to run off the road to avoid a collision, earth banks and ditches are far safer to hit than poles or trees. If it is impossible to run off the road, turn your vehicle at an angle to avoid a head-on collision.

CUTTING RIGHT-HAND CORNERS

Avoid cutting the right-hand corner. This is a dangerous practice because it will put you on the wrong side of the road (see figure 5). Before you turn, make a final right-hand mirror check, in case somebody is foolish enough to overtake you on the right-hand side. Always look into the road you wish to turn into for any possible danger. Remember to look and assess the situation before you decide if it is safe to make any driving decision.

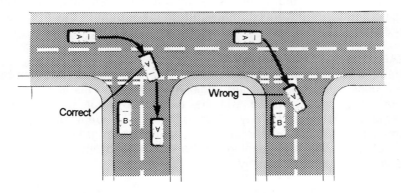

Figure 5. Avoid cutting right-hand corners.

D

DANGEROUS LOADS

Many vehicles carry loads which are very dangerous. These include substances which are corrosive, flammable, poisonous, infectious, radioactive, etc. If you are involved with a vehicle carrying a dangerous load this could result in the death and/or injury of many people. Information about the load being carried must be displayed on hazard information panels on the outside of the vehicle. If you are involved in a crash with one of these vehicles, and the driver is incapacitated, carry out the following procedure:

- Call the fire brigade.
- Do not touch spilled chemicals and avoid breathing any fumes.
- If you are splashed with any chemical, wash it off with plenty of water **immediately**.
- Keep everyone away.

DANGEROUS POSITION
You should always stop your vehicle in a safe, legal and convenient place. It is not only an offence but highly dangerous to leave your vehicle in such a position that it is likely to cause danger to other persons using the road (e.g. parking on a bend).

DAZZLED BY HEADLIGHTS
If an oncoming driver dazzles you with his vehicle headlights, you should slow down, and if necessary, stop. Do not retaliate, and avoid looking directly at oncoming headlights, in case another driver dazzles you again.

DEAF AND HARD OF HEARING
If someone is profoundly deaf or hard of hearing, they must remember to be constantly vigilant at all times when driving. This is extremely important because he/she will be unable to hear either traffic, emergency vehicles or any other danger. The deaf driver must compensate for his or her lack of hearing by a greatly improved perception of what's happening on the road ahead and by observing everything much more closely.

DEALING WITH BLACK ICE
One of the most terrifying experiences whilst driving is to suddenly find yourself driving on black ice. You should be on the look out for these areas and recognise them not only from their appearance but from the actions of other vehicles so that you can take the appropriate precautions in good time to avoid skidding. Remember, tyres travelling on ice make practically **no** noise. Refer to the correction of skids.

DEALING WITH CROSSROADS
It is important to remember that **all** crossroads are dangerous and they must be treated with caution. Although you may have priority, there is nothing to stop a vehicle or cyclist pulling straight out in front of you. You must always take effective observation before emerging. Moreover, there is one particular type of crossroads that are often accident black spots; it is unmarked crossroad. This is potentially the most dangerous type of junction. Some drivers just drive straight through without slowing down, thinking they have priority.

DEALING WITH FIRE
Many serious and sometimes fatal accidents can be prevented by taking correct and prompt action should fire break out in the engine compartment

of your vehicle. Fire can spread through a vehicle in seconds. It is therefore essential that you always carry a fire extinguisher in your vehicle at all times. If you smell burning or suspect that there is a fire in the engine compartment, you must stop your vehicle at a safe place as quickly as possible and switch off the engine. The first priority is for the safety of any passengers who may be travelling in the vehicle with you. Make sure that they all exit as quickly as possible by selecting the safest route and keep them well away from the car. Contact the fire brigade immediately. Under no circumstances open the bonnet wide as you will create a draught of air which will fan the fire and you may cause a mini-fireball. As soon as you open the bonnet slightly, direct your fire extinguisher through the small gap and fully extinguish the fire. If you do not have a fire extinguisher in the car, avoid opening the bonnet and call the fire brigade instead.

DEALING WITH LEVEL CROSSINGS
Many drivers and their passengers have been killed at railway level crossings. Always approach and drive over a level crossing with vigilance and caution. A driver should never enter a crossing until the road is clear. It is of paramount importance to avoid driving too close to another vehicle over the level crossing.

It is also important that the driver should never stop on or just after the crossing, or park near the level crossing. If your vehicle breaks down, or if you have an accident on a railway crossing, you must carry out the following procedure **immediately** to remain safe.

- Get everyone out of your vehicle and tell them to stand a safe distance from the crossing.
- Look out for a railway telephone and use it immediately to tell the signal operator your predicament.
- Follow the instructions given by the signal man.
- If it is practical (providing there is time), before a train arrives, move your vehicle clear of the crossing.
- If you hear an alarm or see an amber light, abandon your vehicle and move quickly away from the crossing.

DEALING WITH ROUNDABOUTS
When you approach a roundabout, look well ahead for the advance warning signs. These signs will depict the layout of the roundabout, show route directions, and give you advanced warning of the appropriate traffic lanes at the roundabout. You should select in good time the most appropriate lane in which to approach the roundabout. Do not straddle or change lanes at the last moment.

Gently reduce the speed of your car. Start looking early to your right, in order to monitor the amount of traffic already on the roundabout, as well as other vehicles emerging into the roundabout. If it is not safe to proceed at the roundabout, you must stop and give way. Remember a give way sign means give way. You do not have to stop, only stop if it is necessary. If you stop needlessly, you may hold up other traffic, causing inconvenience or even an accident (see figure 6).

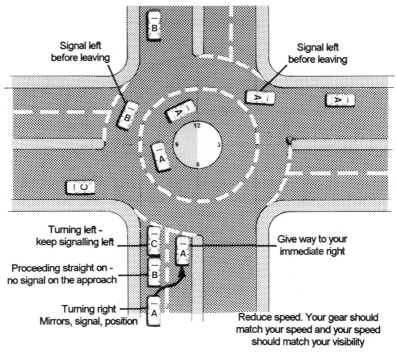

Figure 6. Dealing with roundabouts.

When you are looking to the right at a roundabout it is important that you use peripheral vision so that you can keep an eye on the vehicle in front, in case it stops without warning. Many accidents occur this way. You must always look forward and check that the vehicle in front has definitely moved away before you enter the roundabout. Remember, larger vehicles, especially Large Goods Vehicles (LGV's drawing trailers), require more berth. They may have to manoeuvre into an unusual position whilst negotiating a roundabout.

A word of warning: a driver's zone of vision on the approach to a roundabout can be obstructed by road-side furniture, so be careful. You must always **STOP** and give way to traffic from the immediate right, if you are in any doubt. Finally, don't assume when driving on a roundabout that you will continue to have priority, you may occasionally see traffic lights, road signs or markings telling you that you have to give way to other traffic. So be careful.

DEALING WITH TRAFFIC ACCIDENTS

No matter how carefully you drive, or what preventative measures you take, short of keeping your vehicle in your garage, there is always a risk of being involved in an accident, caused by the stupidity, carelessness or inexperience of someone else. There are three general groups of factors which contribute to accidents:

- The vehicle.
- The driver.
- The environment.

Out of these three categories, driver error is responsible for most traffic accidents which result in someone being injured. In a recent survey carried out in the UK, nine out of ten road deaths and injuries are caused by **men**, one third of whom are below the age of 21. The survey also revealed that 95% of all accidents are caused by driver error. Many people panic or freeze when they are involved in a traffic accident. If you are involved in a traffic accident, always keep calm and carry out the following procedures:

1. **Stop** at the scene, and remain there for a reasonable period if any person has been injured or if there is damage to any other vehicle, property or licensed animals.
2. Switch your engine off; ask other drivers involved to the same.
3. Extinguish cigarettes - there may be petrol leakage.
4. Tell your passengers to leave your vehicle and get them to a place of safety. If any of your passengers are seriously injured, it would be wise to leave them in the vehicle and administer first aid.
5. Warn other traffic.
6. Call the ambulance service and the police.
7. At night make sure that no one stands at the rear of your vehicle as they may obscure the lights. You can also use your lights to illuminate the scene. Vehicle indicator lights or hazard warning flashers will alert oncoming traffic.

8. Try and move any vehicle if it is causing danger to other traffic, ask an independent person to note the original positions of vehicles.
9. Exchange your registration number, insurance and address details, and if different, that of the vehicle owner, to anyone who has reasonable grounds to ask for those details.
10. You must, if injury is caused to another person, produce your certificate of insurance either to any other person who has reasonable grounds or to a police officer.

If for any reason you do not comply with the above, you must report the accident at a police station or to a police officer as soon as reasonably practicable or within 24 hours. You must also report if another person was injured and you did not produce your certificate of insurance at the time. If the certificate is not available you must still report the accident, but can produce the certificate to the police within seven days. If there is an allegation or possibility that your vehicle's presence on the road was a factor you must also comply with the above. Your insurance details can be requested if someone else holds you responsible for the accident. This can be made at a later stage and does not have to be at the scene of the accident.

You can purchase a special hammer with a chromium-plated head and a razor-sharp blade so that you can shatter the side window of your car and cut the seat belt if you are trapped during a crash. The hammer comes with a plastic holder which is easily attached inside the car. It also has a fluorescent knob so that you can locate it more easily in the dark.

DEALING WITH TRAFFIC LIGHTS
Far too many road accidents are caused by drivers ignoring a red light and wrongly crossing your path. It is important that you observe traffic lights early and treat them with caution. Don't forget to regulate your speed correctly on the approach, and always take effective observation before emerging, in case you have to stop. Furthermore, if the traffic lights fail, proceed with extreme caution.

DRINKING AND DRIVING
In a survey carried out in the United Kingdom, one in five deaths on the road were caused by drivers who had been drinking. Many drivers mistakenly believe that they are safe to drive because they have only consumed a very small amount of alcohol. In fact, even the smallest amount of alcohol can increase a driver's reaction time and cause them to misjudge distance and the speed of oncoming vehicles.

Alcohol also gives a false sense of confidence, which encourages drivers to take risks and drive at speeds inconsistent with safety. Various circumstances can account for the variation in time it takes to metabolise alcohol. Some people have more effective livers than others, but the combination of height, weight and body water content is an acknowledged factor.

It has been medically proved that alcohol is quickly absorbed into the bloodstream, which affects the brain and impairs driving ability. Drivers also have a greater tendency to endanger their lives, particularly in dangerous manoeuvres such as overtaking. Drinking and driving is irresponsible and extremely dangerous. Remember, someone may be driving with their alcohol level at nearly zero and driving perfectly legally, but their performance is still less than it would be, if they had not been drinking at all. The only way to stay alive is **not** to drink and drive.

Reasonable suspicion and roadside testing
There has been much talk of the so-called practice by some police forces of random breath-testing and its legality. In fact under the present state of the law, a random breath test is illegal. This is because the police would have no reasonable suspicion of the existence of any of the facts which would entitle them to administer a breath test. However this is seldom a problem for the police as a constable is empowered to stop any driver in order to inspect his licence, MOT certificate and insurance. If in so doing, the constable's suspicion is aroused reasonably, for example if he smells alcohol on the driver's breath, then a breath test can be legally demanded. Similarly, unusual or erratic driving may create a reasonable suspicion in the police that alcohol has been consumed so that a breath test can again be required. The police also have a blanket right to call for roadside tests following a road traffic accident. It is clear then that successful defences based on the request for a breath test, will be few and far between.

The roadside test is a fairly basic screening exercise designed to filter out those who are clearly over the legal limit from those who are not. A breath test should therefore be distinguished from breath analysis which will give an accurate indication of actual alcohol content. There are several approved devices in current use which all have slightly different instructions. For example, if you have smoked a cigarette within the last 10 minutes or consumed your last drink within the last 20 minutes you should tell the police officer. It is likely that you will have to wait for a short time before taking the test.

If you fail this roadside test, usually evidenced by a series of red or red and amber lights, then you will be arrested and taken to a police station for a proper breath analysis. If you refuse to provide a specimen of breath for a roadside test without reasonable excuse, an offence will have been committed which carries 4 penalty points and discretionary disqualification. The defence to not providing a roadside specimen is "reasonable excuse". However, in general unless there is evidence of a physical disability or other medical complaint, it will be no reasonable excuse that you tried as hard as you could.

If you have been involved in an accident and the police suspect that someone else has been hurt, they are empowered to go into your home, if necessary using reasonable force, to further their investigations. Generally, the roadside screening device is an accurate piece of machinery whose parameters are so widely drafted that they leave little room for error and therefore challenge.

At the police station
If the roadside test suggests that you may be over the legal limit to drive, an evidential breath specimen will then be required. The printout it produces is good evidence and will be used in court. There are several "approved" devices, but the Camic and Lion Intoximeters are most widely used. By this stage the police should be following a strict procedure book. This details the calibration of the breath testing equipment and the method of taking the sample itself. Failure to comply with the correct procedures may well provide the basis for a sound technical defence. Indeed, over recent years many prosecutions have failed because of procedural non-compliance. However after each case, the loopholes become ever more difficult to wriggle through as amending legislation is introduced.

Two samples of breath are required. The lower reading will be used in any legal proceedings. For **breath, the legal limit is 35 µg of alcohol in 100 ml of breath**. In practice, to allow for machine error, the police will not pursue you if the reading is between 35 and 40 µg. If between 35 and 50 µg, the police **must** offer you the opportunity to have your blood or urine analysed. A failure to explain this will amount to a defence. Again, a fair body of case law has evolved in respect of this legal requirement.

As a result, it is now clear that the police must offer you either blood or urine. It is the offer of the option which is critical but this is somewhat farcical as once the offer has been given, it is the police who can decide which sample to take and send off for analysis. Their decision will be based upon the equipment available at the respective station. In the majority of cases, blood will usually be taken. You will also be given a sample and details of an independent testing laboratory to obtain a detailed analysis. Only in very rare cases will the police and your own analysis differ. If blood is to be taken, it can only be with your consent and by a police surgeon. If you are convicted of an offence, you may be required to pay the doctor's fee. *The limits are:* **80 mg of alcohol in 100 ml of blood and 107 mg of alcohol in 100 ml of urine.**

driving on the continent. They usually offer a full range including fire extinguishers, warning triangles, first aid kits and headlight beam reflectors. It is also important to remember that in some Islamic countries there are different laws regarding women driving. You can be at your most vulnerable to muggers when you are driving in known tourist areas.

Attacks usually happen when driving a rented car because the attackers can then easily identify you as a tourist. If you are hiring a car at your vacation destination, avoid collecting it at night but instead hire a taxi to your hotel or apartment. When you collect the car the following morning, plan the safest route back and take time to familiarise yourself with the location and function of the car's minor and auxiliary controls. Always check to see how much fuel is in the tank before leaving the rental company's premises. Moreover, try not to dress like a tourist. Hide your wallet or purse in concealed, zipped or button pockets. Try not to dress conspicuously - that means Hawaiian shirts, shorts and sandals especially when it is raining.

The Channel Tunnel
The Channel Tunnel is a remarkable feat of engineering. Journey time between platforms is 35 minutes, 27 minutes being underground. There is a 24 hour service, loading and unloading time can take 8 minutes and at peak times there is a 'ferry' service every 15 minutes. However, there is trepidation in the minds of many motorists regarding the safety of the tunnel which are unfounded.

The tunnel is buried 150 feet beneath the seabed for most of its route and is bored through a thick, watertight layer of chalk. Drivers sit in their cars, although you may leave your car if you wish. An aerial built along the length of the tunnel allows people to listen to their car radio and a ventilation system has been designed to extract car fumes rapidly.

In the event of fire, foam-injection systems and fire extinguishers are activated. Even if these fail, passengers are able to pass through a fire barrier to another carriage. The carriages are designed to withstand the worst blaze for at least 30 minutes allowing the train to reach one of the terminals. Each carriage has two emergency doors wide enough for wheel-chairs. If the fire was so bad that the train could not be moved, passengers are able to walk safely through cross-passages leading into the service tunnel. Security measure include the routine use of electronic devices capable of detecting plastic and other types of military explosives, and X-ray machines located at each terminal will screen vehicles. The guard has full video surveillance and each carriage has an alarm button.

DRIVING AT NIGHT

When you are driving at night, you will not be able to see as far as you can in daylight, especially whilst driving in heavy rain. Driving under these conditions requires extra care because your vision will be severely reduced to the front, rear and sides of your vehicle. You should always be particularly mindful of pedestrians who are either walking with their heads down or fail to look in either direction when it is raining heavily or during any severe weather conditions. Remember that your judgment of the speeds of other vehicles will be impaired since you have only their lights on which to base your judgments.

It would be prudent to put on **your** lights before lighting-up time if you are driving a dark coloured car. Do not be embarrassed to be the first driver to switch on your headlights. Remember, it is better to *see and be seen*. When you are driving out of a brightly lit area (tunnel or underground car park etc.) you should drive with extreme caution to give your eyes time to adjust to the darkness.

Night driving requires a great deal of tolerance and restraint. The oncoming driver who fails to dip his headlights may be either inexperienced, or elderly or nervous, and any attempt to intimidate him by pulling over towards the oncoming driver or by angry light flashing and horn beeping might result in serious consequences.

Allowance must be made for cyclists who do not make themselves visible by wearing light coloured fluorescent clothing and cyclists riding without front or rear lights or a red rear reflector.

You should 'dip' your headlights early when meeting other vehicles, and when following another vehicle, care should be taken to avoid your light beam being reflected in the mirror of the vehicle ahead.

If it is necessary to carry out repairs, you should move your vehicle off the road, if possible. Remember that it is an offence to park your vehicle on the right-hand side of the road facing oncoming traffic during the hours of darkness without showing two white lights to the front and two red lights to the rear.

You should be constantly on the alert for vehicles with either no lights, or one light deficient, or very dim and dirty lights. Also watch out for unlit vehicles parked on dark roads. Be particularly mindful of pedestrians who may be wearing dark clothing and therefore may be obscured.

DRIVING INTO DEEP WATER

If your car should happen to crash into deep water and become totally submerged, it is highly important to remain calm during this emergency. You should allow your car to fill with water until the level is almost at the top. You should then take one last gulp of air before opening the door or window and swimming to safety. You will be unable to open the door prior to this because of the pressure difference, and if you open the window too early, too much water would gush in at once.

DRUNKEN PEDESTRIANS

We are all aware of the dangers and consequences of drinking and driving. However, another menace on the road is the drunken pedestrian. In a survey of traffic accidents involving pedestrians in the United Kingdom, a quarter of these pedestrians were found to be under the influence of alcohol. They wander or stagger off the pavement onto the road, into the path of vehicles, causing them to swerve. Swerving suddenly to avoid a pedestrian can be highly dangerous, as you may hit or be struck by another vehicle overtaking you, or you may even collide with oncoming traffic. You should therefore apply good forward planning whilst driving and be particularly mindful of drunken pedestrians who may step out from behind parked vehicles without warning. Remember that when you are approaching parked vehicles, always look underneath them so you can see if there are feet moving behind. Watch the behaviour of drunken pedestrians at all times so that you can anticipate their actions and stop safely. Take extra care at night, especially when passing places where people socialise and drink.

E

EMERGING SAFELY AT GIVE WAY JUNCTIONS

Another area of driving fraught with danger is emerging from give way junctions. It is very important to know what you are looking for before emerging at a give way junction. You must look out for and give way to other vehicles, cyclists and pedestrians who may be using the road into which you are turning. Motorcycles tend to travel very fast and their riders do not always make themselves visible by wearing brightly coloured clothing. Remember as you look left, to check for any vehicles which are overtaking and are on the wrong side of the road.

Do not forget that parts of your car obstruct your view so take this into consideration at all times. Watch out for any vehicles that may be emerging from a side road or drive way. They may be hidden by parked vehicles or road-side furniture. A good tip is to wind your window down, (especially in fog or at night) and listen for approaching traffic (see figure 7).

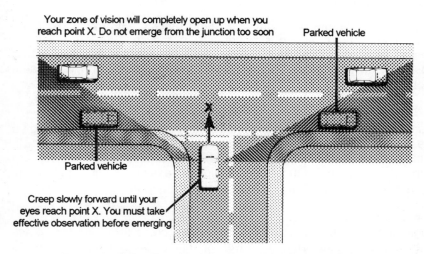

Your zone of vision will completely open up when you reach point X. Do not emerge from the junction too soon

Parked vehicle

Parked vehicle

Creep slowly forward until your eyes reach point X. You must take effective observation before emerging

Figure 7. Emerging safely from give way junctions.

EMERGENCY VEHICLES

If you see blue flashing lights or hear the siren of a police, fire brigade, ambulance or any other emergency vehicle, you must take whatever action if possible, with safety, to allow that vehicle clear passage. However, if you come across the incident the emergency vehicle is attending, don't rubberneck! (Turning your head round and staring at the accident with a morbid curiosity). You must concentrate on what is happening ahead or you could cause another accident.

ENGINE FAILING

If the engine seizes up, this may be due to overheating caused by a broken fan belt or lack of coolant. Complete seizure results in the driving wheels locking. De-clutch immediately and move the gear stick into neutral. Check the mirrors, signal and move the side of the road, making sure not to cut in front of other vehicles.

F

FIRST AID

Many people die in the first few minutes after a traffic accident. To help save lives think of *ABC*.

A = Airway

Unconscious people can choke to death quickly. Gently tilt the head back and remove any obstructions from the mouth. If the injured person is lying outside the vehicle, turn him or her into the "coma position", on their side. This will allow the injured person to breathe more easily.

B = Breathing

Listen for any signs of breathing. If you do not hear any breathing, give the injured person mouth to mouth resuscitation ("The Kiss of Life"). This can be carried out in the vehicle. However, if victim(s) are trapped, mouth to mouth resuscitation is easier to carry out if the injured person(s) are lying on their back on the ground.

C = Circulation

Look where the blood is coming from, then press firmly on that place with a clean handkerchief, towel or piece of clothing. Points to remember:

- If the injured person is unconscious and there is no danger of the vehicle catching fire or being struck by another vehicle, you should leave them in the car. Moving them may make internal injuries and fractures worse.
- Always move the head and neck as gently as you can. Ask someone else to assist you.
- Do not give the injured person any alcohol. This can make bleeding worse and increase strain on the heart.

FIRST AID KIT

Every vehicle should carry an extensive first aid kit. It is important that you read the instructions on the kit when it is first obtained. It should be kept clean and closed and stored in the glove box, instead of the boot, which may be unreachable in the event of an accident; any items used should be replaced. Remember, whilst driving abroad certain countries make it an offence **not** to carry a proper first aid kit.

FLASHING YOUR HEADLIGHTS

Headlights can also be used as a signal to warn other road users of your presence; e.g. during the hours of darkness, flashing your headlights can be a useful warning before overtaking another driver, or during daylight hours, you may flash headlights instead of a horn warning on motorways or any other fast roads (where owing to the speed of the vehicles, other drivers may not hear the horn). Flashing your headlights means exactly the same as sounding your horn, i.e. it lets other road users know you are there. Do not flash headlights to another driver or pedestrian for any other reason. It is dangerous, for example, to "flash" other drivers to emerge from a side road - they must be allowed to use their own judgement on when it is safe to do this.

FLOODED STREETS
On the approach to flooded areas, always drive through water at a very slow speed in a low gear. It would be prudent to leave your car and check the depth of the water and also for any hidden obstruction or subsidence. If the water is deep, slip the clutch and apply the accelerator to keep the engine running fast. Check your brakes afterwards to ensure that the brake linings are dry.

G

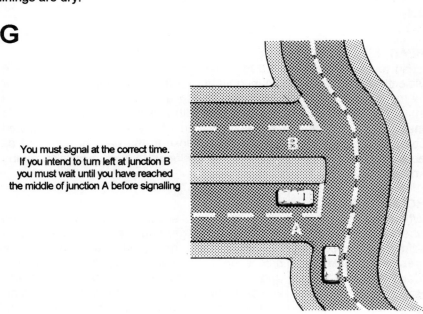

You must signal at the correct time. If you intend to turn left at junction B you must wait until you have reached the middle of junction A before signalling

Figure 8. Giving proper signals.

GIVING PROPER SIGNALS
If you give any signal it must be given in good time, in a clear and unmistakeable manner. You must signal if it would help other road

users, including pedestrians. Many accidents are caused by drivers and motorcyclists signalling incorrectly and at the wrong time. Remember the routine, Mirrors, (Look Assess Decide), Signal, Manoeuvre (see figure 8).

Making proper use of your mirrors and applying good forward observations when driving, will avoid late and unnecessary signalling. Always check that your signal has been cancelled after any manoeuvre; if you fail to do this, other road users might misinterpret your intentions and an accident could occur. A word of warning - never emerge from a "give way" junction if you see another driver signalling his intention to turn.   It is prudent to wait until you receive more positive information before emerging, i.e. wait until the other driver slows down and makes a definite move to turn. He may have left his indicator on by mistake.

H

HEAD RESTRAINTS
Head restraints are designed to prevent the occupants heads from being violently jerked backwards during an impact (to avoid whiplash injuries), or thumped from the rear passengers during a frontal collision. It is highly important that anyone sitting in a seat with a head restraint fitted should make sure that the top of the rigid part of the restraint is positioned correctly at or above eye level and as close to the back of the head as possible. The restraint should also be designed to stay in position during impact, that is, not push down or rotate.

HOLDING BACK
When dealing with potentially dangerous situations, there will be times where you should "go" (in other words, get your vehicle to an area of safety), situations where you cannot "go" (and may have to be prepared to take defensive action) and finally, situations where you "don't know". The "go" and "don't go" situations are self-explanatory. However, if you come across actual or potential danger on the road whilst driving and you feel you do not have enough information to make the correct driving decision, then you must hold back until you receive more knowledge of the road situation so that you may make the correct decision.

Make sure you gauge the length of the vehicle you wish to overtake. If the vehicle you are overtaking is a Large Goods Vehicle, you should hold well back to give yourself the best possible view past the lorry so that you can overtake once you can see that there are no hazards ahead (See figure 9). Be very careful, because large vehicles can often obscure hazards. If you gauge the length of the vehicle correctly, you will be able to judge how much further you will have to travel before you can safely pull back onto your side of the road. Always consider the speed of an oncoming vehicle before you decide to overtake. For example, imagine you are travelling at 50 mph and an oncoming vehicle is doing the same speed; you are approaching each other at 100 mph or 150 feet (46 metres) per second!

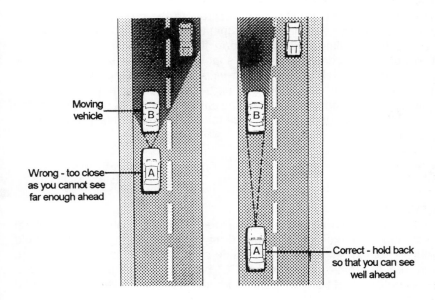

Figure 9. Hold well back.

HOSTILITY

You should never drive in a way which provokes reaction from other drivers. For example: do not hog the right-hand lane (policing the road) - someone may wish to overtake you. Although you may be driving to the maximum speed limit, other drivers may want to go faster and staying in the right-hand lane may result in open hostility, abusive language, threats, physical violence or worse! If another driver wishes to exceed the speed limit then that is his problem if he gets caught breaking the law!

J

JOY RIDERS
The media is full of stories of the modern-day menace on the roads - joy riders. Joy riders are usually young men who may be high on drugs or alcohol and steal cars for kicks, destroying and dumping them later. They drive erratically and at great speed, without regard to their own safety or the safety of others. Should you come across joy riders whilst travelling on the road, you should avoid them at all costs and not confront them. You should, however, record the registration number, a description of the vehicle and occupants and the direction in which the vehicle is travelling and then inform the police as soon as possible. The police nowadays have very sophisticated means of tracking joy riders, such as helicopters armed with infra-red cameras, etc. Police nowadays can stop joy-riders in their tracks with a remote control gun. This device can cripple a car engine within a radius of several hundred yards. The gun uses similar technology to the Tracker car tracing system.

K

KEEP ALERT
When you are overtaking a Large Goods Vehicle, a big lorry or driving past high walls, keep both hands firmly on the steering wheel to avoid your car being "knocked" by any side draught. Take special care when you see a vehicle displaying an "L" plate or a foreign number-plate. This could indicate an inexperienced driver or one unused to driving on the left-hand side of the road.

KEEP CALM
Always be patient and tolerant whilst driving behind the wheel. You are most likely to have an accident when you are angry or tense. Similarly, anything that you do to irritate another driver will increase the likelihood of an accident. If another driver shows lack of care or good manners, do not retaliate.

KEEP YOUR DISTANCE
Many road accidents are caused by drivers getting too close to the vehicle in front. On the open road, in good conditions, always keep a safe distance from the vehicle in front: a distance of one metre for

each mile per hour of your speed or a two-second time gap, in case the driver ahead brakes suddenly. This will also leave space for an overtaking vehicle to pull in. On wet or icy roads, the gap should at least, be doubled. In any case, this is a sensible precaution to prevent road accidents. Drop back if an overtaking vehicle pulls into the gap in front of you. If you do not leave enough distance from the vehicle in front, you will make it easier for the other driver to force you to stop, and if you are rammed from behind you will have no escape route (see figure 10).

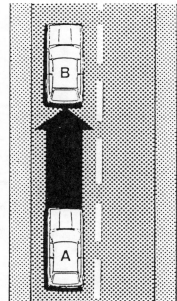

Figure 10. Keep your distance.

KILLER OVERTAKE

Many serious and fatal accidents are caused by the killer overtake. Some drivers perform the killer overtake unintentionally - whilst attackers can use it intentionally. This scenario occurs when the driver in front moves out to overtake another vehicle and you follow behind him (even after first checking the road ahead is clear far into the distance). When he is just past the vehicle he is overtaking, he then waits in the same position level with this vehicle on the inside until another vehicle appears in the distance heading directly towards him. The driver will then accelerate past the vehicle he is overtaking and move quickly into the inside lane. You will then be left to collide with the oncoming vehicle (see figure 11 and two-second rule).

You must be aware of the acceleration capability of your car so that you can move out of the "danger period" as soon as possible. Overtaking could be the last decision you will ever make if it is the wrong one. *Remember the golden rule*; "If in doubt, Don't".

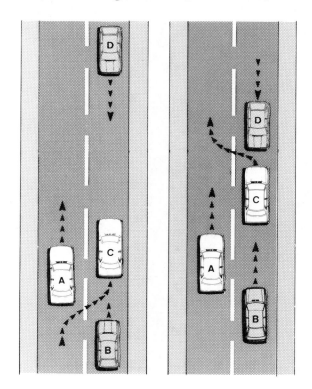

Figure 11. The killer overtake.

L

LIGHTS FAILING
If both headlights suddenly cut out, slow down quickly. Use any other source of illumination you have, e.g. fog lights, spot lights or emergency four-way flashers. They can all help you to drive at a slow speed to safety.

LOOSE WHEELS

If 'clanking' noises are heard, this may be due to loose wheel nuts. Slow down gently, stop and retighten the nuts. As a precaution, drive to a convenient garage where a mechanic can check the wheel, its nuts, bolts and wheel bearings. If the wheel comes off, the car will drop at the affected corner, resulting in a strong pull to one side. Counter this by firm steering and gentle, progressive braking to bring the car to a halt. One important point; refrain from overtightening the wheel nuts as they may become impossible to loosen in an emergency.

M

MACHO DRIVER

The problem with many young male drivers is that they feel under pressure from their friends and their culture in general to be aggressive and macho when driving. Such ideas are reinforced by computer games which encourage young boys to overtake at great speeds and generally risk their "lives" for high scores. This behaviour is not conducive to sensible driving when they come to face life on the real roads. When they "die" playing the computer game, they lose one "life"; on the real roads, they only have one life (See figure 12).

Figure 12. The macho driver.

MAKING PROGRESS

It can be highly dangerous not to make proper progress. Other drivers may get frustrated and take silly risks to overtake you, if you do not make normal progress to suit varying road and traffic conditions. There are two main instances of this. The first is that you are travelling too slowly for the road and traffic conditions. For example, if you are driving along a road at 20 mph, when it has a 30 mph speed limit and you could easily travel safely at 30 mph, you may inconvenience other road users for not making progress. Effort must be made by you to use the accelerator to build up the speed of your car, changing up through the gears where necessary. You must endeavour to keep up with the flow of traffic, within the speed limits. Do not reduce speed too early on the approach to a turn, as other vehicles may dart in front of you. Avoid weaving in and out between parked vehicles at short intervals (see figure 13).

Figure 13. Making progress.

MAKING PROPER USE OF MIRRORS
Many accidents are caused by drivers not making effective use of their mirrors. Before you make any driving decision, the first thing you must do is check your mirrors. The mirrors are the eyes in the back of your head. Effective use of mirrors means looking and acting sensibly on what was seen. In other words, you must Look, Assess and Decide. Do not drive with blind eyes. When you look at your mirrors, avoid staring at them - you only need to take a quick glance. If you take your eyes off the road for more than a split second, the road situation ahead could have changed and an accident may occur (see figure 14).

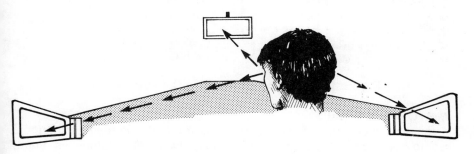

Figure 14. Making proper use of mirrors.

MEAT IN THE SANDWICH
When you are driving on a narrow road, you may come across a situation where you will meet other vehicles. This situation usually arises when driving in a built-up area and ahead of you, you can see there are two parked vehicles, one at the left-hand side of the road and the other at the right-hand side, possibly directly opposite each other. This can be termed a "bottleneck". A problem arises when you see another vehicle approaching, and because of timing, it is obvious that both vehicles are going to reach the bottleneck at the same time. The one thing you must not do is speed up and try to get through the gap before the other driver. This is very dangerous because the other driver might do the same and this often results in an emergency stop being carried out at the last moment or something worse. *There's an old saying, "Never be the meat in the sandwich"*. Never be the idiot to get caught in between two vehicles, anything could happen and you will be trapped with no place to go. A good driver always looks well ahead and scans the area for any possible signs of danger and acts as the situation demands (see figure 15).

Figure 15. Don't be the meat in the sandwich!

MOTORWAY DRIVING
Every year thousands of people are killed or maimed in road accidents. Some horrendous accidents occur on motorways. On motorways, you will be driving at very high speeds, especially if driving abroad. High-speed motoring is safe if it is carried out with skill and responsibility.

Before driving on the motorway
Before you decide to drive on the motorway, it is imperative that you check the general condition of your car, because you will probably be driving at high speeds. You should always check that your tyres are in good condition and the tread depth is within the legal limit. It is important that your tyre pressures are set correctly. Make sure you have enough fuel and oil, and also check the water levels. Ensure your windows, headlights, indicators and mirrors are clean. If you are drawing a trailer, check and secure the load before commencing your journey. If you feel tired or unwell do not under any circumstances drive on the motorway. You may fall asleep and possibly kill yourself or someone else.

Feeling tired
If you ever feel tired whilst driving on the motorway, wind your window down for ventilation and leave the motorway at the next exit or the nearest service station. In a detailed survey carried out in the UK and the USA, researchers found that many motorway accidents were caused by drivers falling asleep at the wheel. Most accidents happened

between 4 am and 6 am. The investigators also found that sleep-related accidents were three times more likely to result in serious injury or death than any other road accident. This was because sleepy drivers failed to brake to try to prevent the accident - so the impact was worse. Their study also revealed that many drivers found long distance motorway driving very monotonous. This caused them to daydream whilst driving, often going into "trances". In fact, the survey also revealed that many long distance drivers had absolutely no recollection of large parts of their journey. Many drivers who fall asleep at the wheel include shift workers who constantly sleep for short periods and drivers who embark upon long drives in the morning with insufficient sleep the night before. Remember, "*Stay Awake, Stay Alive*".

Using the hard shoulder

If something falls off your car when driving on the motorway, move over to the hard shoulder as soon as it is safe. Many pedestrians are killed or seriously injured whilst standing or walking on the hard shoulder. Try to position your car as far over to the left hand side of the hard shoulder as possible. Warn any passengers of the dangers of passing vehicles and place a warning triangle approximately 150 metres (165 yards) to the rear of your car. This will help to prevent you from being struck by another vehicle which may be positioned badly in the left-hand lane. Look out for a telephone symbol with an arrow to tell you where the nearest emergency telephone is (these telephones are directly connected to a police control room). Do not under any circumstances cross the central reservation to use an emergency telephone.

When rejoining the left-hand lane, build up your speed first on the hard shoulder. Wait for a safe gap in the traffic, and signal if necessary before emerging. Watch out for any motorway speed restrictions or flashing light signals which will warn you of any hazards ahead. You will usually see them on overhead gantries or at the side of the carriageway. If you ever see any flashing amber lights, check your mirrors, and if it is safe, use progressive braking to slow down (especially in poor weather conditions) until you are satisfied that it is safe to go faster again.

N

NEGLIGENTLY OPENING CAR DOORS

Such accidents are all too common, and a court would have no hesitation in determining that the car driver (or passenger) was negligent in not checking that the road or pavement was clear before opening the door into the path of a passing cyclist or pedestrian who was injured or if there was danger of injury. Therefore, before opening a car door always check to make sure that you are not endangering any driver, cyclist or pedestrian.

O

OVERALL STOPPING DISTANCE
Imagine that you are driving along a quiet road at 30 mph, in good conditions, and all of a sudden, someone pulls out in front of you. By the time your brain acknowledges this information and you react by braking to a stop, you would have travelled a distance of approximately 23 metres (75 feet). On a wet, slippery road, it is double the distance.

OVERTAKING OTHER VEHICLES SAFELY
Most fatal traffic accidents are caused by overtaking, because you will be driving on the wrong side of the road, towards oncoming traffic. It is therefore crucial that you only overtake when it is one hundred per cent safe to do so. Never overtake unless you are sure there is no danger to others as well as to yourself. Before you start to overtake, make sure that the road is clear far enough ahead and behind you. Remember to use the Mirrors (Look, Assess, Decide), Signal Manoeuvre routine. On fast roads, vehicles may be coming up behind much more quickly than you imagine. Also, make sure that the lane into which you intend to move is clear far into the distance. When overtaking cyclists always give them plenty of room, as they have a tendency to wobble, swerve or change direction without warning. Before overtaking any vehicle, you must ask yourself the following questions:

1. *Would I be breaking the law if I overtake?*
2. *Can I overtake safely?*
3. *Does my car have enough speed and power to overtake?*
4. *Can I safely get back into my own lane in time?*
5. *Do I have a safe gap to get back in?*
6. *Is it necessary?*

Remember the golden rule, *"If in doubt, DON'T"*.

Overtaking with determination
Look well ahead for oncoming traffic, junctions or hazards before you decide to overtake. If it is completely safe ahead, behind and to the

sides of your car you should then overtake the vehicle with determination. Remember, you are on the wrong side of the road and the less time you spend there the better. Hold a parallel course until the vehicle you have overtaken is visible in your interior mirror. By doing this, you will have moved back in well ahead of the overtaken vehicle and you will not have caused it to slow down or change direction. This will also allow space for another overtaking vehicle to pull in. There is no need to signal your intention to move back in after overtaking because other drivers would expect you to drive on the left-hand side of the road anyway. Signalling left could make other drivers or pedestrians mistakenly believe that you intend to turn left (if there is a side road ahead) or stop on the left-hand side of the road. Signalling for the sake of signalling is a dangerous practice. Check your mirrors and increase a gear, conditions permitting.

P

PARKING ON HILLS
Here are some safety precautions you can take when parking on up and downhill gradients.

Parking facing uphill
Try and stop your vehicle as close as you can to the nearside kerb. You should then turn your steering wheel to the right. If your vehicle rolls backwards, the front wheels will be halted by the kerb. However, if there is no kerb, you should turn your steering wheel to the left to prevent your vehicle rolling backwards across the road. Finally, always leave your vehicle in first gear with the parking brake securely on in case the parking brake cable snaps.

Parking facing downhill
You should turn your steering wheel to the left. The kerb should stop your vehicle from moving forward. In light of this, you should also leave your vehicle in reverse gear with the parking brake securely on.

PARTIAL OR TOTAL LOSS OF SIGHT IN ONE EYE
If you suffer from loss or partial loss of vision in one eye, moving off from the side of the road can be hazardous. You will lack peripheral vision, and must therefore look all round over the shoulder to overcome this problem. Additional mirrors may also be used to give you a much better field of sight. When the car is moving it is essential

that you move your head more in order to see what is happening around you.

It is permissible to quickly glance over your shoulder before you decide to change direction to the right or left, to check for other road users in the blind spot especially motorcyclists, before joining a motorway or duel carriageway from a slip road and acceleration lane. However, if you find it necessary to check your blind spot on the move, you must be extremely careful because a vehicle in front may make a quick lane change or break sharply when you are looking over your shoulder and not at the road in front.

PASSING A STATIONARY VEHICLE

When approaching a parked vehicle make sure you carry out the Position, Speed, Look - Mirrors (Look, Assess, Decide), Signal, Manoeuvre routine as previously mentioned. You must Look, Assess and Decide if it is completely safe before you decide to pass any stationary vehicle. It is of the utmost importance that you check your mirrors early. You must look well ahead. If it is safe, move out from the obstruction as early as possible, leave plenty of room, and watch out for pedestrians who may step out from in front of parked vehicles.

Before passing a stationary vehicle, always look underneath it so that you can see if there are feet moving behind. Watch out for the parked vehicle's door opening, and keep a good safety line position. The safety line position is the safest position to adopt on the road, in relation to the actual and potential danger existing at that moment. Actual danger when passing a stationary vehicle could be a person sitting in the driving seat of his car who may decide to open his car door without looking. Potential danger could be passing a parked vehicle from behind, where a pedestrian could walk out in front of it.

PATIENCE

Never be tempted to turn or move out from a road junction because an impatient motorist has beeped his horn at you. Use your own judgement as to when it is safe. Try, however, to anticipate a safe gap in the traffic and emerge at the earliest opportunity to avoid upsetting other drivers.

PLANNED DRIVING

There will be occasions when time spent on planning your route will prevent you from getting lost and you will be in a better position to deal with any hazards which may lie ahead. When your car is in motion, always keep an eye on what other drivers are doing and be aware of the general road and traffic conditions. Make full use of peripheral vision to avoid eye contact, as this may attract attention. However, you must avoid "information overload", in other words you must not become overwhelmed with so much information that you fail to observe any real danger at all. A poorly organised visual search system will be inefficient in collecting relevant information in sufficient time to react safely if you are attacked. It may also cause you to over-react to an incident where there is no real danger.

S

SEAT BELTS
Wearing a seat belt is not just a legal requirement - it makes good sense. Research shows that a person not wearing a seat belt can be seriously injured or killed in a crash when a vehicle is travelling at speeds as low as 12 mph. If a baby is travelling in the car with you, make sure that you use an approved baby carrier suitable for the child's weight. Failing to wear a seat belt may also affect your claim for compensation if you are involved in an accident.

SHATTERED WINDSCREEN
If your windscreen shatters when you are driving, you should punch a hole in the windscreen wide enough for you to see through. This will enable you to carry on driving until you decide it is safe to stop. If loose chippings are being thrown up at your windscreen from the road surface or from a passing lorry, the best protection to stop you windscreen from shattering is to place the fingertips of one of your hands hard against the glass. This absorbs the impact.

SKIDDING
There are three different types of skids that may occur if you are driving a motor car: a front-wheel skid, a rear-wheel skid and a four-wheel skid. There are four main causes of skidding: excessive speed, harsh braking, fierce acceleration and erratic steering. A good driver never gets caught in a skid. If you are looking well ahead and driving at a speed appropriate to the road and traffic conditions, a skid will never happen.

The correction of skids
If your car gets involved in a skid, you must know what caused the skid and the most effective way to correct it. As soon as you apply harsh pressure to the footbrake the occupants and the full weight of your car are thrown

forwards, making the rear of your car much lighter. When this happens the rear wheels could lose their grip on the road. If you apply too much pressure on the accelerator the occupants of your car are pressed back in their seats, making the weight of your car much lighter at the front, and the front wheels could lose their grip on the road. If your car is cornering too fast, the occupants of your car are thrown sideways and a skid could again occur (see figure 16).

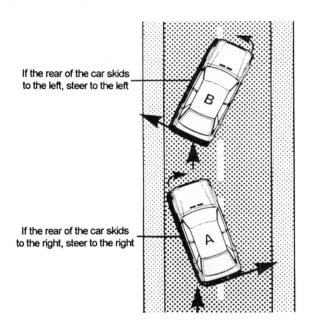

If the rear of the car skids to the left, steer to the left

If the rear of the car skids to the right, steer to the right

Figure 16. The rear-wheel skid.

The front-wheel skid

A front-wheel skid normally happens on a bend or corner when the front wheels of your car lose their grip on the road, and the car does not travel in the direction you intend. As soon as you realise this is happening, release the footbrake immediately and re-apply the footbrake more gently, straightening the steering to allow the front wheels to regain their grip on the road. Then steer to a safety line position.

The rear-wheel skid

If your rear wheels lose their grip on the road, and the rear of your car swings either to the right or to the left you are in a rear-wheel skid. It is normally caused by harsh braking or excessive speed for the road conditions. As soon as you realise this is happening you must take your foot off the brake pedal, and turn the steering wheel in the direction of the skid. If the rear wheels slide to the right, turn the steering wheel to the right. If the rear wheels slide to the left, turn the steering wheel to the left. When you have gained full control, you can then steer your car to a safety line position.

The four-wheel skid

Finally, if all four wheels of your car lose their grip on the road, you are in a four-wheel skid. This occurs if you apply the footbrake too suddenly and you will feel the car sliding helplessly out of control in any direction. To correct this type of skid you should relax the pressure on the footbrake. This will allow the wheels to re-grip the road and then pump the brake pedal on and off (rhythmic or cadence braking) until you regain control.

Anti-locking braking systems (ABS)

If your vehicle is fitted with anti-lock brakes, they can be extremely useful in an emergency. When the wheels are about to lock, a sensor control releases the brake and applies it again, which is really automatic rhythmic braking. In other words, you can keep the pressure on and steer at the same time.

SNOW

Weather conditions can alter rapidly during winter months. \If your car gets bogged down in heavy snow and you cannot break free, it is crucial that you know how to survive until help reaches you. It is best to prepare for the worst as you may have to wait for some time. The will to survive varies considerably in human beings, but evidence shows that some individuals have been able to survive extreme winter conditions for very long periods of time. The most fatal mistake is to leave your engine running continuously, as you may fall asleep and then, because of the sudden cold, die without recovering consciousness if the engine cuts out or runs out of fuel. It is safer to switch the engine off and on periodically in order to conserve petrol. To survive severe winter conditions you should keep the following points in mind:

- Have and maintain a positive mental attitude.
- Push negative thoughts out of your mind and conserve energy.

- Exercise to prevent painful stiffness and to maintain body warmth. This must be carried out slowly and frequently to conserve energy and should not be overdone.
- Protect the body from cold and damp.
- Guard against boredom and depression. Keep yourself and any passengers occupied .
- Unless you know for a fact that help is at hand, do not wander off in search of food. You may get frostbite or hypothermia.
- Ration any food that may be carried in the car.
- Light a fire as soon as possible. Ideally, light three fires in a triangle shape (this is an international distress signal). Consider using your car's cigarette lighter if you have no matches .
- Write the word "HELP" on the snow in very large letters to it can be easily seen from the air.
- Cover your vehicle and the aerial with brightly coloured items so that you can be seen from the air by any rescue team. Remember to brush off any snow covering frequently.
- Never eat snow or ice as it will reduce body temperature and cause sore lips, gums and tongue. Always use melted snow or ice.
- Remember, in cold areas exposure causes death before lack of fluids or food. Many deaths in the middle-aged and elderly are caused by strokes and heart attacks brought on by exposure to the cold. Research shows that within half an hour of considerable cooling of the body, blood becomes more liable to clot. Anyone suffering from exposure should be provided with heat as soon as possible.

Before setting off on your journey during severe weather conditions always ask yourself is your journey absolutely essential?

You should carry the following equipment in your car if you believe there is any possibility of blizzard conditions:

1. Emergency food and water
2. Spare fuel
3. Shovel
4. Snow chains
5. First aid kit to include water purification tablets and lip balm
6. Knife and torch
7. Sleeping bag(s) or blanket(s)
8. Metal container for heating food and water
9. Map
10. Mobile phone

Moving off in deep snow

If you are starting off in deep snow and you encounter wheel spin, do not race the engine because your wheels will dig in further. To overcome this problem you should move your car slightly backwards and then forwards until you break free. Use the highest gear possible. In these conditions, it is a good idea to carry a spade and place old sacks or car mats under your wheels so that your tyres can grip more easily, to stop your car being embedded in the snow. Always remove any heavy snow lying on top of your vehicle before moving off. When you brake, weight is transferred to the front of your car; any snow that has not been cleared from your vehicle's roof may suddenly fall onto the windscreen and your vision will be severely restricted. Many accidents have occurred in this way.

SOUNDING YOUR HORN

You can use your horn as a signal to attract the attention of others. Always sound your horn if you have reasonable cause to do so. For example, suppose you are parked at the side of the road between two vehicles and the vehicle in front starts reversing towards you. If you believe it is not going to stop, then in these circumstances it is in fact permissible, on account of the danger, to sound the horn to warn the other driver.

STEERING FAILING

If you feel an increase in steering wheel movement, or steering 'wander' when attempting to steer a straight line, you should have your steering checked by a qualified motor mechanic as soon as possible. However, a sudden jolt to severely worn steering joints could cause them to separate, resulting in steering failure. Do not execute an emergency stop but brake firmly and progressively until your vehicle comes to a complete halt.

STOPPING IN AN EMERGENCY

If you have to stop your vehicle in an emergency, the amount of pressure you apply on the footbrake will depend on the road conditions. If the road is good, firm and dry, you can push the brake pedal harder as the car slows down. However, if the road surface is wet and loose, you will have to brake less firmly. If the brake is applied too hard, you may skid. Moreover, your brakes can be your worse enemy on wet or icy roads. If you can't stop in time it may be better to steer carefully round something than to slide into it. Remember if your brakes and tyres are not in first class condition you will take longer to stop.

SURVIVING IN FOG

Fog is one of the most dangerous weather conditions in which to drive. Some drivers drive at very high speeds, even though their visibility is seriously reduced and some horrific accidents occur. Thick fog is always dangerous and the best possible advice for driving in thick fog is, **DON'T**.

However, if your journey is vital, be extremely careful when you are driving in these conditions. By viewing Teletext/Ceefax or contacting any of the major motoring organisations, you may be able to vary your route to avoid the worst of the fog. If this is not possible, drive by the route which is most familiar to you. Driving in fog can cause eye strain and your ability to anticipate the actions of other road users will be severely restricted, so you must:

- Check your mirrors and slow down. Keep a safe distance. You should always be able to pull up within your range of vision.
- Don't hang on to someone else's tail lights - it gives a false sense of security.
- Watch your speed; you may be going faster than you think. Do not speed up to get away from a vehicle which is too close behind you.
- Obey any warning signals. They are there to help and protect you.
- See and be seen. Use dipped headlights or front fog lights. Only use rear fog lights when visibility is severely reduced. Use your windscreen wipers and de-mister.
- Check and clean your windscreen, lights, reflectors and windows whenever you can.
- Remember that fog can drift rapidly and is often patchy. Even if it seems to be clearing, you can suddenly find yourself back in thick fog.
- Drive in the left-hand lane of the motorways and dual carriageways as much as possible.
- Open your window(s) so that you can hear any approaching traffic and keep your foot on the brake pedal (an extra warning for drivers behind) if you are waiting to turn at a road junction. Consider using your horn to warn other road users of your presence.

T

TRAMS

Trams are being reintroduced into cities throughout the UK to both provide a more efficient public transport system and a more environmentally friendly form of transport. Trams have been found to encourage tourism and commerce as a result of their convenience and safety. Here is a check list of do's and don'ts that will both help you to keep safe and maintain the smooth running of the tram system:

Do

- Exercise care until you and other drivers are familiar with a different traffic system.
- Treat crossing points the same way as railway crossings.
- Be careful when turning or braking on the steel rails as they may be slippery even when they are dry.
- Obey all signals. Diamond shaped signs give instructions to tram drivers only. When there are no signals, always give way to trams.
- Watch out for trams that run close to the kerb or where the lines move from one side of the road to the other.
- Stop for additional pedestrian crossings where passengers will be embarking and disembarking from the trams.
- Be particularly mindful of cyclists and motorcyclists. Their narrow tyres may put them in danger when in contact with the rails.

Don't

- Try to race trams. If you need to overtake, remember that the trams may be as long as 60 metres (200 feet). Try and overtake at stops if it is safe to do so.
- Drive between platforms at tramway stations. Follow any direction signs.
- Park where your vehicle will obstruct trams or other road users.
- Enter reserved areas for the tramway which are marked either with white line markings or a different type of surface, or both. These are often 'one way', but occasionally 'two way'.
- Be caught out by the speed and silence of the trams.

TRAPPED INSECT

If you are driving and you notice an insect such as a bee, wasp or hornet trapped inside your vehicle, do not lash out with your hand. This will only antagonise the insect. Open a window so that it can fly out - if this fails, pull into the side of the road and open the door.

THE TWO-SECOND RULE

Imagine you are following a vehicle and it has just passed a roadside feature such as a lamp-post in the pavement. If you reach the lamp-post before being able to repeat slowly, *"one second, two seconds"*, then you are driving too close to the vehicle in front.

TYRE BLOWOUT

If one of your tyres blows out, the car may pull to one side. The risk is increased if the brakes are applied. You should grip the steering wheel firmly, take your foot off the accelerator and roll the car to a stop by the side of the road at a safe and convenient place. Remember, if you use hard braking, this will only make things worse. Before you attempt to change the wheel, always move your vehicle to a safe and convenient place first. This is a sensible precaution to take as you may expose yourself to danger from other vehicles. Always carry a legal spare tyre and proper equipment to change a tyre at all times.

V

VEHICLE COMBAT

You should, at all costs, avoid getting into a situation where you may come across a driver who will try to antagonise you into "vehicle combat" or competitive driving. This type of driving creates dangerous situations; for example, the other driver may prevent you overtaking by cutting in front of your vehicle or he may slam on the brakes suddenly. Alternatively, he may try to goad you into racing against him when you are stopped at traffic lights. Such drivers often undergo a severe personality switch, changing from a person of quite normal disposition to an irrational psychopath! If you come across such a driver, you should restrain yourself from involvement in this for obvious reasons.

W

WINDSCREEN WIPERS FAILING

If your windscreen wipers suddenly stop during heavy rain, keep driving straight ahead. Crouch over the wheel and place your face close to the windscreen so that you can see where you are going and pull into the side of the road as soon as possible.

WINTER MAINTENANCE VEHICLES

In wintry weather conditions, winter maintenance vehicles spread rock salt across the road as a precaution against ice patches or snow accumulations. These extremely powerful machines are designed to spread salt across all lanes of motorways and major trunk roads. If you come across one of these vehicles whilst driving on the motorway, you should hold back and maintain a safe distance behind it. Remain very patient and **do not** attempt to overtake the maintenance vehicle because salting operations are based on well-planned routes and the vehicles, which usually travel about 35 mph, will most probably leave the motorway in a short while. You should also take special care to watch for irregular build-up of snow caused by ploughing operations and **never** attempt to overtake snow ploughs by squeezing into partially cleared lanes.

WINTER SUN DAZZLE
Dazzle from the sun during the winter is an underestimated hazard. If this happens to you, reduce your speed and use your sun visor to minimise dazzle and to prevent you driving with 'blind eyes'.

WORN SHOCK ABSORBERS
Worn shock absorbers can seriously affect your vehicles handling. Worn shock absorbers allow the wheels to bounce excessively on the road surface. Therefore, road contact is insufficiently maintained resulting in decreased tyre-to-road grip. An excellent way to check for worn shock absorbers is to press down heavily on each wing in turn. The car should bounce once and then return to a stable position. Moreover, if your car is three years old or it has clocked 40,000 miles, it would be prudent to have your shock absorbers checked by a competent mechanic.

Z

ZEBRA CROSSING
The zebra crossing is normally marked by zig zag lines on both sides of the crossing, with flashing beacons at either side of the pavement, black and white panels running across the length of the road and rows of studs along the edge of area to be used by pedestrians. So there is no excuse for not seeing them.

When approaching a zebra crossing, the Mirrors (Look, Assess, Decide), Signal, Manoeuvre routine should be applied. Check the mirrors early so that the situation behind you may be assessed and allow you time, if necessary, to roll down your window and give a slowing down arm signal. This is a very important signal to give because it both warns following vehicles of your intention to slow down and gives pedestrians confidence that you are preparing to stop your car for them. Stop just before the white give way lines and give children and elderly people plenty of time to cross. Do not rev your engine as this may frighten them.

You must not overtake either the moving motor vehicle nearest the crossing or the leading vehicle which has stopped to give way to a pedestrian on the crossing. Even when there are no zig zag lines, never overtake just before a zebra crossing. In traffic queues, leave pedestrian crossings clear.

Chapter 6

Evasive Manoeuvring Techniques

If you have followed all the advice given in this book so far, 99 times out of 100, you will enjoy trouble-free motoring. However, there may be an occasion where you find your route blocked, for whatever reason, and the following manoeuvres may prove useful in this situation.

THE J-TURN

If you cannot mount the kerb to drive round the hazard because of road-side furniture, you could carry out the J-turn. The J-turn will only succeed if the exit to your rear is **not** blocked. We shall now examine how to handle the car during this exercise. Imagine your car is in fourth gear and that you are travelling at 30 mph (see figure 17).

Making effective use of mirrors

Before you can make any safe driving decision, the first thing you must do is check your mirrors. The mirrors are the eyes in the back of your head and must be checked well in advance. Late use of the mirrors will lead to poorly organised and hurried driving decisions. A good driver will always know what is behind him and what is happening around the sides of his car.

Speed

If it is safe and the exit to your rear is not blocked, the next thing you should do is stop the car quickly and under control. To achieve this, you should be pushing the brake pedal harder as the vehicle slows down and try to stop well before the hazard if you can. Keep both hands on the steering wheel (because you will need as much control as possible) at the "ten to two" or "quarter to three" position (avoid wrapping your thumbs round the rim).

Escape route

As soon as you come to a halt, you must again look in the rear-view mirror. Avoid staring at it as you only need to take a quick glance in case the situation behind you has changed. If it is safe, you should now take hold of the gear lever firmly and select reverse gear, positively and distinctly, without looking down at the gear lever. After selecting reverse gear, you should return your hand back to the steering wheel and reverse quickly under full control. If you cause your wheels to spin, you will lose valuable time. You must coordinate the use of the foot and hand controls so that you move the car smoothly and accurately.

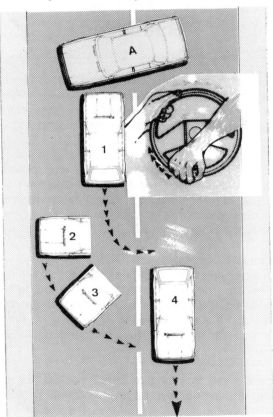

Figure 17. The J-Turn.

Palm-down, thumb-down position

When you are reversing rapidly under full control, imagine the steering wheel as a clock face. Place your right-hand in a position on the steering wheel, at seven o'clock. This technique is known as the "palm-down, thumb-down" position. When the car has built up sufficient momentum, take your foot off the accelerator and turn the steering wheel to the right as quickly as possible. Imagine throwing the steering wheel out the window. The weight of the engine will drag the front of the car round (anti-clockwise), and you will end up facing the opposite direction.

Position
When the car is almost in its new position, take hold of the gear lever firmly, and quickly select first gear whilst tensing your right hand to give you more control of your steering. After you have selected first gear, you should return your hand back to the steering wheel and, using the foot controls smoothly, keep full control of the car when accelerating away.

THE TWO-POINT TURN
The two-point turn basically achieves the same result as the three-point turn, but does not take as long to carry out. Imagine you are driving along and the road ahead of you is effectively blocked. It is impracticable to implement a J-turn because you cannot build up sufficient momentum in reverse gear. In this situation, you will find the two-point turn manoeuvre useful for turning within a limited space. The idea of the manoeuvre is to turn your car round to face the opposite direction using reverse then first gear. Since this manoeuvre has to be done quickly, you must be able to control your car and coordinate your clutch, accelerator and steering together (see figure 18). The best way to remember how to do this manoeuvre is to split it into three stages. Remember the following code:

- PREPARATION
- OBSERVATION
- MOVE

Stage 1: *Preparation*
Immediately you stop your car before the obstruction, you must select reverse gear. As soon as you have selected reverse gear, apply the accelerator and quickly let the clutch out until the engine note changes - **feet still**.

Stage 2: *Observation*
Quickly turn well round in your seat and look out the rear window because that is the direction in which the car will travel.

Stage 3: *Move*
Providing that the road is clear, begin to move the car back quickly. Choose a place where you have plenty of room, and where there are no

obstructions in the road or on the pavement. Turn the steering wheel as far to the right as possible (full right lock) and aim to get your car at a right-angle across the road. As the car crosses the crown (middle) of the road, push the clutch down as fast as possible and brake stopping the car before the kerb. You should try to turn the steering wheel at least once to the left so that by the time your car stops, the wheels are straight ahead or possibly with a partial left lock on. Apply the parking brake quickly (if you are on an incline) and select first gear as fast as possible. Then move off to the left under full control without stalling or causing excessive wheel spin. **Remember the rule: "Keep the feet slow and move the hands fast".**

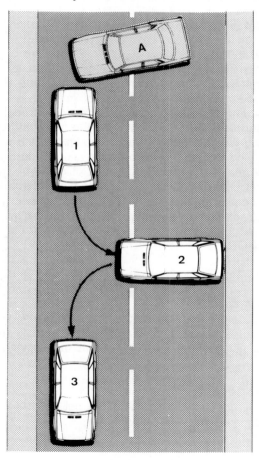

Figure 18. The Two-point turn.

TO SUM UP
You must remember to calculate the camber of the road so that you will be able to judge how much power your car will need for the manoeuvre. In most roads, for drainage purposes, the highest point is in the centre (or crown). The crown slopes at either side down to the gutters and the degree of slope from the crown to the gutters is known as the camber.

Some cambers are quite steep, other cambers are so small that, to all intents and purposes, you could be on level ground. It is obvious that the steeper the camber you are on, the more throttle will be required in order to keep good control of your car.

THE BOOTLEGGER TURN
If you find yourself in a situation where the road ahead of you is effectively blocked, another option open to you is the bootlegger (or 'U') turn. The idea of this manoeuvre is to turn your vehicle completely round within the width of the road without reversing. The bootlegger turn should only be attempted in a wide, quiet road (see figure 19).

Imagine that your car is in fourth gear and you are travelling at 30 mph and someone pulls out in front of you. The best way to remember how to do this exercise to split it into three stages.

Stage 1: *Speed*
As soon as you can see the obstruction ahead, you should apply the footbrake. Don't check the mirrors - there is no time (you should know what is behind you if you are checking your mirrors properly). The footbrake should be pressed firmly and progressively, but under full control, to reduce your speed to approximately 20 mph.

Stage 2: *Gear*
When you have your speed completely under control, change directly from fourth gear into second gear. Second gear should be selected in enough time to allow you to turn the car around without striking the obstruction. The clutch at this point must be brought fully up which will assist you in braking and help keep the car under control. I cannot stress enough that the clutch must be brought fully up throughout this manoeuvre -if you don't you will not have maximum control of your car.

Stage 3: *Escape Route*
If you are driving on the left-hand side of the road, turn the steering wheel briskly to the right and position the car right round in the width of the road (or vica versa). It is vitally important that you keep braking continuously throughout the manoeuvre until the car is turned around in the direction

you wish to go. As soon as you have positioned your car correctly, you should apply gentle pressure on the accelerator and take the correct safety line position in your new road. If you do not apply gentle pressure to the accelerator you may encounter a front or rear-wheel skid. Always remember the sequence, **"brake before clutch"**. This manoeuvre can be hazardous because you may have to cross the path of oncoming traffic.

Figure 19. The bootlegger turn.

THE HANDBRAKE TURN

One other manoeuvre which can be undertaken is the handbrake turn (see figure 20). By pulling the parking brake up sharply and suddenly whilst the car is in motion and turning the steering wheel hard to the left or right, the car will immediately spin round in that direction. However this is a very difficult manoeuvre to perform as control is almost completely lost and it is impossible to know which direction your car will be facing when it stops spinning, especially in wet conditions (if you keep your foot on the accelerator the car will spin for longer). Other manoeuvres described in this book are usually preferable in the vast majority of situations.

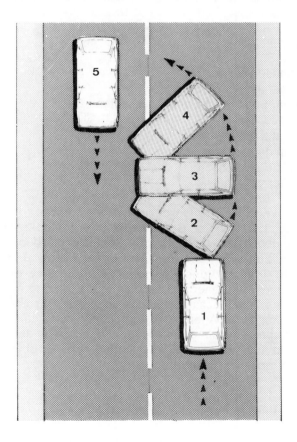

Figure 20. The handbrake turn.

MORE FROM OTTER PUBLICATIONS.......

BUYING YOUR NEXT CAR: your questions answered (1 899053 07 7, 96 pp, £3.95) is packed with essential information which will help all would-be car buyers of second-hand cars make the right decision. Given that buying a car is the second most expensive purchase that an individual will make, it is vital to get it right. This book contains over one hundred questions. *DON'T BUY A USED CAR UNTIL YOU HAVE READ THIS BOOK - IT MAY WELL SAVE YOU POUNDS!* The key areas covered include:

- How to choose your car
- Finding a genuine used car
- The structural and mechanical assessment
- The test drive
- Used cars and the law
- Coping with dealers and sellers
- Motor vehicle auctions
  Looking after your 'new' car

BEHIND THE WHEEL: the learner driver's handbook (1 899053 04 2, 264 pp, £7.95), also by *Graham Yuill*, is a step-by-step, highly illustrated handbook. Now into its fourth edition, the book **features a full colour section and questions and answers to help the learner driver learn to drive and pass the theory driving test.** *BEHIND THE WHEEL* will teach the reader all aspects of driving and road safety in 20 easy lessons The teaching methods used are those laid down by The Driving Standards Agency. A completely up-to-date section on trams has also been included. Finally the events of the driving test day are outlined in full with useful advice and tips. **Endorsed by the Driving Instructors Association.**

"Anyone who is learning to drive, or teaching someone else, will appreciate Behind the Wheel". *Woman and Home.*

"Learner drivers will find this publication an invaluable aid not only in learning to drive safely, but also in passing their theory and practical driving test". *John E. Ayland, Chief Examiner DIAmond Advanced Motorists, formerly Deputy Chief Driving Examiner, Driving Standards Agency.*

DRIVING FOR INSTRUCTORS: a practical training guide (1 899053 09 3, £7.95 128 pp) *Graham Yuill*, is a handbook for both experienced and new driving instructors to help them pass the upgraded ADI check test. The teaching methods used are those laid down by The Driving Standards Agency. **Endorsed by the Driving Instructors Association.**

"This guide is a must for potential and fully qualified Approved Driving Instructors. There is a wealth of information here for those who wish to improve their instructional skills". *John E. Ayland, Chief Examiner DIAmond Advanced Motorists.*

WORKING FOR JUSTICE: the employee's guide to the law (1 899053 06 9, 224 pp, £7.95), aimed at all employees, is a guide through the many legal aspects of working for somebody else. Given the uncertainties of modern employment contracts, a well-informed knowledge of the law as it affects us is critical. The easy to understand language makes the book extremely accessible and a helpful glossary of terms explains the legal jargon used. *WORKING FOR JUSTICE* is intended as a practical handbook. The key areas covered include:

- Employment status
- Pay
- Unfair dismissal
- Wrongful dismissal
- Redundancy
- Disciplinary matters
- Discrimination
- Trade Union membership
- Maternity
- Health and safety
- Transfer of undertakings
- Employment law in Northern Ireland

How to order:-
Through your local bookshop or in case of difficulty, please send a cheque made payable to Otter Publications, 5. Mosse Gardens, Fishbourne, Chichester, West Sussex, PO19 3PQ, ☎ 01243 539106.